EQUALITY IN MANAGING
SERVICE DELIVERY

Rohan Collier

OPEN UNIVERSITY PRESS
Buckingham · Philadelphia

Open University Press
Celtic Court
22 Ballmoor
Buckingham
MK18 1XW

email: enquiries@openup.co.uk
world wide web: http//www.openup.co.uk

and
325 Chestnut Street
Philadelphia, PA19106, USA

First Published 1998

A catalogue record of this book is available from the British Library

ISBN   0 335 19730 2 (hb)   0 335 19729 9 (pb)

Library of Congress Cataloging-in-Publication Data
Collier, Rohan, 1945–
    Equality in managing service delivery/by Rohan Collier.
        p.   cm.
    Includes bibliographical references and index.
    ISBN 0-335-19730-2 (hardcover). – ISBN 0-335-19729-9 (pbk.)
    1. Customer services – Moral and ethical aspects – Great Britain.
2. Discrimination – Great Britain.   I. Title.
HF5415.5.6623   1998
658.8′12 – dc21   98–9786
                                                                                                        CIP

Typeset by Type Study, Scarborough, North Yorkshire
Printed in Great Britain by Biddles Ltd, Guildford and Kings Lynn

EQUALITY IN MANAGING
SERVICE DELIVERY

CONTENTS

PREFACE

Equal opportunity is now an integral part of the work of many organizations. However, adoption of equalities into everyday management remains patchy, and in my experience is much more likely to be developed in areas of employment than service delivery. But limiting equality principles to employment is irrational; there are equally compelling arguments for equalities to apply to those an organization serves. It is this area of equalities, that is equalities as they relate to service delivery, that *Equality in Managing Service Delivery* aims to address.

The book is largely based on my own experience. I first faced issues relating to service delivery as an elected councillor and chair of a 'Women's Committee' in an inner London borough in the 1980s, trying – not always successfully – to move the council from concentrating on women's employment issues towards looking at service delivery issues as they affected women in the borough. Since then it has become a recurring issue as I have worked for the voluntary sector and in local government. On each occasion it has been important to make the organization aware of its responsibilities to those it serves, to see the advantages of recognizing the rights of its customers, and to search for ways of listening to their needs. Often special strategies have been needed to develop these relationships. Sometimes it has meant developing new ways of reviewing services from an equalities point of view, using new devices for monitoring and consultation. It has also meant overseeing a programme of change designed to increase the organization's responsiveness to citizens' needs. Here the problems surrounding ways of assessing the needs of the citizen (customer) have to be tackled. My own experience in these developments has come from over ten years working mainly in local councils (first as an elected member, then as an equalities officer) but also in the voluntary sector. My knowledge of the private sector comes from the many occasions when I have dealt with companies either as a trainer, as a negotiator or as a customer. Many of the examples used in the book arise from my work in local government. Often they reflect shared experiences and so material discovered during meetings or discussions. Wherever possible I have given the source of the examples; however, in a book reflecting personal experience and where the field is new, references to published work are often not possible. Inevitably, as the field of *Equality in Managing Service Delivery* matures, references to published work will grow.

Rohan Collier

ACKNOWLEDGEMENTS

In preparing the material for this book, I owe a debt of thanks to both the London Borough of Hounslow and the London Borough of Croydon. Most of the thinking behind this book and its contents were developed as part of my work in these two organizations. Much of the material used in the book is reproduced with their permission. Thanks in particular to my colleagues in both boroughs who contributed to the material of the book. My thanks also go to other agencies with whom I have worked, in particular the police divisions and the health authorities in Hounslow and Croydon boroughs. They too have been a source of inspiration for ideas within the book. Thanks to the Commission for Racial Equality for permission to reproduce 'Give Racism the Red Card' and to Marks and Spencer for reproduction of passages from *Equal Opportunities and You: A Guide for All Staff*. My thanks also go to my colleague Kerstin James for encouragement and comments on early drafts, to Maree Gladwin for comments on the first three chapters, and to Davina James Hanman for sending me numerous examples of equalities in service delivery. Finally, I owe a huge debt to both Joe Collier and Kathy Meade, who have patiently commented on drafts of the text and improved it considerably.

INTRODUCTION

This book looks at equal opportunities in service delivery. It focuses on how services can be tailored to meet different needs. The bulk of work on equal opportunities over the last few decades has been on employment. It has aimed at ensuring that more women, black and minority ethnic people and disabled people are represented at all levels in the workplace. In general service delivery has been ignored. The overall aim of this book is to enable those responsible for designing and managing services to ensure that the services serve the widest number of people and do not discriminate against any particular group. More specific objectives of this book are to give those responsible for the delivery of services an understanding of:

- discrimination and how it affects those who face it
- the law as it relates to discrimination
- how 'equalities' fits into the government's drive for 'Best Value'
- how to develop and implement equal opportunities policies in the delivery of services
- how to measure success and analyse failure.

The target audience of this book is those responsible for serving the public, including decision makers, change agents and managers in services run in the private, public or voluntary sectors. Most examples in the book are from local government, some are from the health service, and others from the private sector where equalities in service delivery is developing fast, particularly in the retail sector.

Principles on which this book is based

What counts as a service?

There is no easy answer to this. It is probably most satisfactorily defined as the provision or supply of goods or facilities that individual people, or the community at large, need or want. A service is different from a 'product' that a consumer might buy. A product, such as a television, is taken from the retailer and brought home for use. A service is, for example, the one provided by the retailer selling the television. A service is intangible and its production is inseparable from its consumption. This is why it is difficult to provide a 'measure' or standard for services (see Chapter 6). Services vary enormously across sectors and within the same sector. Some are paid for directly by the customer using a sports centre or buying goods in a shop. Others are paid for through taxes by government or local government – use of highways, use of parks, refuse collection. Some are freely chosen – whether to use a swimming pool or buy some goods; others are not – few people choose to have their children taken into care. Some services are reserved for certain groups of people – nurseries for under-fives, sheltered housing for vulnerable adults; others are open to all – open spaces, sewerage, pedestrian crossings, telephone services. Some services have a quasi-judicial nature – planning permission, police; others have legal statutes associated with them – education for 5- to 16-year-olds, the provision of housing to homeless families; others are entirely up to the provider – community centres, entertainment. Some public sector services run similar services to the private sector – sports centres, schools; others are entirely run by the public sector – street cleansing (even if con-tracted out). Differences between public and private sector provision of services are becoming blurred as more and more services are either contracted out or directly run by the private sector. Some services are used by one person – retail, leisure; others by a whole community – street lighting. Some people are direct customers – a pupil at a school; others are indirect customers – future employers of that pupil. In all sectors there is a difference between actual customers – those who use the service, and potential customers – those who at present don't use the service but could do so. It is the needs of potential customers to whom much of this book is addressed. Some people are eligible for a service but do not use it because of various barriers operating to exclude them (these could be information barriers – the service is only advertised in English, or physical barriers – it is only available up a flight of steps and so on). Barriers to access to services are looked at in Chapter 2. There is also a difference among existing customers using the same service, some of whom may not be treated in the way they need and are therefore getting an inferior service. These are the groups of people equal opportunities is about.

What is equal opportunities?

For the purposes of this book 'equal opportunities' or what is now often referred to as equalities is defined as people's right to equal value in terms of services – that services should be fair in the way they are distributed and not be to the advantage of any one group. There are, however, exceptions to this when services are specifically targeted toward certain groups. For example 'meals on wheels' are targeted at frail older or disabled people; however in this example the service can still unfairly discriminate. The service should be equal in the sense that different groups of older or disabled people – for example different ethnic groups – should have equal access to the service. On this definition 'equality' (the right to services of equal value) therefore depends on the recognition that people have different needs. This is the principle on which this book is based.

The meaning of other terms used in this book will be as follows: 'gender equality' refers to equal opportunities between women and men; 'race equality' refers to equal opportunities between people of different ethnic origins. 'Black and minority ethnic people' will be used to mean anyone who faces discrimination because of their ethnicity (for example Asian people, African people, Caribbean people); 'disabled people' will mean those experiencing discrimination on the grounds of disability; 'older people' those experiencing discrimination on the grounds of age; and 'lesbians and gay men' those who face discrimination because of their sexuality (please note, the terminology used in quoted material may differ from this). A more detailed discussion on language is found in Chapter 2.

Historical overview

Although the idea of equal opportunities has been around for a long time, work in equal opportunities proper started in the 1970s following the black movement, the women's movement and the first equalities legislation (see Chapter 3). In the 1960s there had been some activity but then equal opportunities was about raising awareness. Those working in equal opportunities were on the whole community activists concentrating on civil rights and attempting to create a sense of social responsibility by changing people's attitudes to the world rather than looking at the way people operated at work. During the 1970s the focus of equal opportunities work moved to institutions where local government became a pioneer in equal opportunity initiatives. This section therefore covers the development of equal opportunities in local government.

Local authorities appointed equalities officers and some set up special units to co-ordinate equalities work. Lewisham Council set up a 'Race Relations Committee' in 1974 and a 'Women's Sub-Committee' in 1978 to ensure a political structure on equalities to oversee the council's work in this area (see Local Government Information Unit 1995: 3). In the 1980s many different units were set up in local government covering race issues, women's issues, disability issues or lesbian and gay issues. For example, in 1986, 11 inner London boroughs had Women's Committees. Their remit was 'to identify women's needs and interests, and then to work to re-shape the council's own services to meet those. They also consult women, and provide information and resources directly to women in the community . . . The Committees have looked at housing policy, transport, social services policies and identified where they are ignoring women or reinforcing women's problems' (Greater London Council 1986b: 7).

In most local authorities during the 1970s and 1980s, emphasis was placed on employment rather than on service delivery. The reasons for this emphasis seem obvious: first, employment was a contained area and therefore easier to tackle; second, legislation on equalities as it related to employment was much clearer and more focused; third, it made sense to change the profile of organizations from all-white male dominated organizations to something more representative of the community they served. Local authorities led the way in equal opportunities and employment. At the same time many local authorities placed great emphasis on training, particularly awareness training (disability awareness, anti-sexism, race awareness, heterosexism). What this training actually achieved is not clear and some of it was definitely counter-productive, as, for example, when training in the early 1980s made white people feel 'guilty' for society's racism. Perhaps the main effect of the training was to teach managers what was expected of them in terms of what to say about equal opportunities rather than what to do to effect change in practice. Much of the equalities work focused on 'policing' what was happening. Work concentrated on regulatory aspects of equalities, either through compliance with legal requirements (Race Relations Act, Sex Discrimination Act) or codes of practice. At the same time many organizations developed their own rules and procedures. This was a 'coercive' approach to equal opportunities. 'They tended to emphasise the "don'ts", i.e. don't ask the following questions in recruitment interviews; don't call women "ladies"; don't call people with disabilities "the disabled" (Pearce 1995: 6). Definite gains were made, however, for example with the introduction of clear harassment (sexual harassment, racial harassment) policies. In the 1970s and 1980s there was a growth in the number of women and black staff employed, although it is unclear how much this was due to a demand for labour as opposed to equal opportunities policies. Despite some gains, most women and black and minority ethnic people employed in the mid-1990s are in low-paid, low-status jobs and few have been promoted to high grades. For disabled people the position is bleaker, with few represented in the workforce.

During the 1980s there was work on service delivery but it tended to be piecemeal, project-based and without any integrated strategy. It failed to meet the expectations of those working in the field. There were some excellent initiatives in areas such as safety and street lighting, transport, domestic violence, racial harassment and housing policies but fundamentally organizations shifted little. One explanation for this was that equalities issues were seen by most decision makers as of marginal importance. In general equalities work was separate from mainstream work and often concentrated on alternative or separate provision for different groups rather than on an integrated programme. For example, sports centres provided special sports sessions for women, disabled or older people. Such work was often unrelated to any corporate strategy and for this reason was viewed with cynicism by many officers. Officers working in local government did not see it as part of their responsibility or directly relevant to the services they ran. It also meant that equalities was vulnerable and easily dropped when cuts were called for. At the same time projects were set up in the community specifically for women, minority ethnic groups, lesbians and gay men or disabled people. These initiatives were important, highly valued by the community and raised the profile of equal opportunities. Work on equalities in the 1980s was also highly innovative; it was an exciting field to be working in. Many of the progressive changes were produced by individuals, providing books in languages other than English in the library for example, or celebrating festivals such as Diwali in schools. In many respects the work of so many of these initiatives was experimental and sometimes failed, which added to the cynicism with which equalities work was often viewed by local government officers. Much of this led to the 'loony left' label given to councils which were attempting to take account of the needs of the different groups of people in their communities. The difficulties encountered by those working in equal opportunities in the 1980s are summarized in a report by the London Borough of Haringey (1991, Section 2.1: 7) and are attributed to:

- a failure to sort what is meant by equal opportunities strategies and to develop clear policies based on clear definitions.
- a failure of effective communication to local residents. Authorities have very often failed to explain their equalities policies to all local communities. Authorities have not taken the lead on this issue and as a result have often had to contend with and respond to distortion.
- a failure in part to deliver based on false expectations that authorities themselves helped to create.
- a failure of corporate management of equalities issues and officer support structures.

Partly in recognition of these failures, in the 1990s equalities work in local authorities has become more strategic, and structures for delivering the work have involved smaller centralized units supporting the work done by service departments. In general they have concentrated on the day-to-day services the community needs and receives rather than on the needs of the organization, so reflecting the pivotal shift from equal opportunities in employment to equal opportunities in service delivery. The move to diversify services to meet different needs has also developed outside local government. Health providers, quangos (quasi non-governmental organizations such as training and enterprise councils), the police, and most recently the private sector have all begun to embrace the need for equality in service delivery. The private sector may well have avoided developing policies on service delivery in the 1980s because such work was seen in the context of politicized debate (e.g. 'loony left'). It is now clear that the private sector recognizes the advantage of catering for the different needs of different groups of customers and is catching up fast.

Framework of the book

This book is placed in a framework in which the public are viewed as citizens and not merely as customers. The private sector was quick to view the public as customers; this was followed by the public sector. This reflected a change in which the public became the focus for those who delivered services. In the 1990s the public have increasingly been viewed as citizens. This move is described below.

For a large part of its history, the public sector has taken a very paternalistic view of its users: a 'we know best' approach. Now organizations are following the private sector in reaching out to the public rather than expecting the public to accept provision without question. There has been a move towards seeing and treating the public as customers. At the same time front-line staff are being empowered to take initiatives and be more responsive to customer needs. Local authorities, like the private sector, became 'obsessed with customers'. The same move happened in the health service and other public sector organizations such as the police. This 'customer care' approach means being close to the customer, taking a customer-led view of services and trying to put oneself in the customer's shoes when thinking about the way to deliver services. 'The customer knows best', 'The customer is always right' is a common stance. This became increasingly important to local authorities when services were being contracted out to alternative providers and customer loyalty was understandably weak as no effort had ever been made to value the people the local authority served. Local authorities have developed means of getting closer to their 'customers' which have included 'public participation in urban renewal and planning, area management schemes and decentralisation to neighbourhoods, consultation with tenants, women, black and minority ethnic people and other groups' (Local Government Management Board (LGMB) 1991: 3). Cardiff City Council put out a customer care and tenant participation leaflet stating: 'The council wants to hear your views . . . Although there are plenty of "experts" in the Housing Department the best experts are those who receive the service the Council provides.' The leaflet goes on to outline its customer care code of practice:

> We are always looking for ways to improve our service. Whilst we cannot guarantee to satisfy every request, this 'Customer Care Code' sets out the standard of service you can expect from the Council's Housing Department. This includes:
> - We will be helpful at all times.
> - We will deal with your enquiries quickly and with the least possible trouble to you.
> - We will make our replies easy to understand.
> - We will ask your views on ways we can improve the service.
> - We will try to ensure that all people receive the best possible service regardless of who they are.
> - If you write to us you will receive a reply within 14 days if you ask for one.
>
> (City of Cardiff 1994: leaflet no. 8)

This followed the move in the private sector towards 'seeing people as individual customers with power and choice over the type, standard and quality of services they receive' (LGMB 1991: 3). The LGMB draws a distinction between 'customers' who use or receive services, 'beneficiaries' who benefit from services others directly receive (parents benefit from their children being at school) and 'stakeholders' who have some interest in the council's affairs (elected members, staff, voters, local business . . .).

One of the important aspects of seeing people as customers is realizing that this means they should have a choice. The element of choice is important to the customer, for example, 'the ability to choose from a meals-on-wheels menu is a significant event in the life of a housebound elderly person' (LGMB 1991: 17). Knowing what standards to expect and how to complain if these are not met is also important when making choices. This emphasis on the quality of a service and its links with equal opportunities is further developed in Chapter 1. An element of choice is important as it empowers people to be more active in their decisions and lessens their dependence and passivity.

Seeing people as customers is one way of viewing people as citizens. A citizen, in this sense, is seen as 'a free agent with the basic and inalienable right to pursue chosen purposes free from interference' (Prior, Stewart and Walsh 1995: 15). This is the view behind many of the 'citizen's charters' and covering a variety of service provision. In this way 'choice' is what defines a citizen: 'the citizen is empowered as a consumer by being given specific rights: to receive information on standards and performance of services, to have individual needs assessed, to assert choices and preferences, to complain and receive redress' (ibid.: 15). In theory service users, under this model of citizenship, are empowered to choose in a market place of services. The government under Margaret Thatcher and John Major passed legislation to 'institutionalize' choice (see Barnes and Prior 1995: 53). This change occurred within the health service, education and social services. Increased choice was achieved first by privatizing public services, thus creating many providers between which consumers could choose. Second, choice has been increased through the contracting process between the public and private sectors (here those in charge of the service do the choosing of a contractor). Third, within the public sector itself choice has been made possible by introducing 'alternative forms of provision'.

But seeing people as consumers has its limitations as it deals only with those individuals who actively receive the service. With this in mind there has been a general move from consumer to customer and then from customer to citizen. The concept of 'citizen' describes the relationship between the individual, the community and the state and implies rights and obligations. Rights and obligations were in the 'Citizen's Charter' 'recast as the rights of individual consumers, and the obligations of government being seen as tasks of management' (Prior, Stewart and Walsh 1995: 1). In this way citizens are agents of the market rather than members of a community.

This model of citizenship is particularly weak in terms of public services, where choice may be limited by factors such as poverty, illiteracy, or the inability to speak English. Also it does not cover services where there may be no possibility to withdraw from the service: 'those who use local authority services or facilities out of personal choice and in the face of competing alternatives are the exception rather than the rule' (Prior, Stewart and Walsh 1995: 152).

Information is important for choice to be possible, but frequently it is difficult for customers to obtain. Barnes and Prior quote examples where lack of information was seen as the main obstacle to getting access to services. One example comes from the experience of older people in Fife. This showed that the lack of information about the services that would allow people to stay in their own homes was the limiting factor to a satisfactory life in people's experiences of growing older. Even if obtained, information needs to be analysed and interpreted. These are tasks which are complex and not easy to achieve. Using information to choose a school is not straightforward. 'Does a high score on the percentage of pupils achieving GCSE passes indicate that a good quality education is being provided, or that the school is good at "cramming" at the expense of all other aspects of education? Does a good survival rate achieved by a surgeon indicate greater skill, or greater selectivity in relation to who will be operated on?' (Barnes and Prior 1995: 56). Genuine choice in both education and health is rare. With education, choice may be possible for the first child, but for practical reasons second and other children will usually go to the same school as their older siblings.

In acute situations people will not feel empowered or even able to choose; anxiety and urgency get in the way of the desire or ability to choose. Barnes and Prior also add other factors which limit choice in crisis situations: 'A combination of fear, deference and loss of identity make assertiveness difficult for those admitted to hospital for acute care' (ibid.: 57). They add that the possibility of choice is more likely for routine situations. In crisis situations, the assumption is that the occurrence is rare and that choice would be exercised only once. Things may be different for patients with chronic long-term diseases. What people want at times of crisis is trust in the quality and appropriateness of the service they receive: 'at times of crisis the priority for most people will be to receive prompt help which they are confident will relieve their immediate danger; offering people a choice between emergency telephone numbers to call in case of fire or accident would be life-threatening rather than empowering' (ibid.: 57).

Contrary to the view of citizenship described by choice in the market, choice can be disempowering. Apart from problems of information, choice always involves taking a risk. There is no way of being sure that the outcome of a choice will deliver the service that is needed. Barnes and Prior summarize the situations where choice would not be seen as empowering:

- If there is no information, or poor information, on which to base decisions.
- If people have no influence over the options available from which they are invited to choose and their possible actions are restricted to the range of options presented to them.
- If they have no grounds for confidence that what is offered will meet their needs.
- If people are inexperienced or unskilled in making choices.
- In crisis situations where a speedy response is necessary to avoid or minimize harm.
- When it creates a dilemma that people feel inadequate to deal with.
- In situations in which public services are required to intervene in people's lives against their will.

(Barnes and Prior 1995: 55)

The dilemmas quoted above refer to services where an individual's choice might affect the choice or availability of services to others. For example, choosing to go for a private operation and 'jump the queue' will mean that others have to wait longer (see Barnes and Prior 1995: 54).

Barnes and Prior argue that in public services the most important aspect of service provision is not 'choice' but the confidence that one will get what is wanted or needed: 'If a market, or any other system of allocating resources, is able to provide what we want, then the presence or absence of choice is irrelevant. The creation of alternative options – increasing choice – does not automatically add value . . . value, in most circumstances and for most people, attaches not to the activity of choosing but to the good chosen' (ibid.: 54).

There are definite strains on the term 'customer', particularly in its application to statutory services where the element of choice is limited such as in the example quoted above (education and health). This is particularly true of services to older people and disabled people who cannot easily take their custom elsewhere. It is also true of cases where someone may not indeed have any choice at all. There is at present no choice in services such as refuse collection, street lighting or road cleaning. There is often no choice in the health service, some local authority services such as planning applications and in the criminal justice system. Some public services are aimed not just at the individual receiving the service but at the community at large. A decision on a planning application, for example, will take into account wider environmental issues and the impact on the local community. Services may be provided against someone's will: children taken into care, older people put into residential care, offenders sent to prison. 'Users of mental health services illustrate the dilemma most clearly: forms of service delivery based on market-oriented models of "customer" are hardly appropriate to people whose liberty can be deprived by the service provider' (Prior, Stewart and Walsh 1995: 152). Beresford and Croft make a similar point when they say that 'People who use mental health services are no more consumers of them than wood lice are consumers of Rentokil' (1993: xv).

One of the problems with the view of citizenship as defined by choice is that the relationship between provider and service user is often very narrowly defined. It can ignore one crucial aspect: that people may want a say in how a service is run and which services should be provided rather than receive information on the service, on its standards or on the means of redress. The consumer model of citizenship only provides for choice at the point of service delivery. Citizens as consumers only have a say over the 'product', the outcome of a decision and not over the process of decision making itself. Decisions leading to which services are provided are not made public under the model. As we have seen 'choice' can be less desirable than 'trust' in the service. The point of consumption as point of choice is often meaningless. Empowering people through genuine choice involves more than merely choosing the service, it involves being able to choose other parts of the process such as policy making or resource allocations. This is where meaningful choices are made. As Barnes and Prior say, 'if the context of choosing is divorced from the contexts in which power in society is exercised, increasing choice cannot in itself be a means of empowerment' (1995: 55). Ways of empowering users will be looked at in Chapter 4. Leaving out choice at this higher level of decision making makes public accountability less likely: 'the reduction of the role of the citizen to that of customer weakens public accountability because it leads to neglect of accountability for policy' (Prior, Stewart and Walsh 1995: 68).

Chapter 1 gives an analysis of accountability in terms of service provision. User involvement in the point at which service delivery is planned, developed or even to some extent managed requires a wider concept of citizenship.

Thus in the planning of services it is becoming increasingly recognized that it is important to take into account not just the views of individuals who receive the service (customers/citizens) but also of the wider community on whom the service might impact. In the case of a school it is difficult to say who is more important, 'the pupil, the parent, future employers or the wider community' (Prior, Stewart and Walsh 1995: 66). Here the term 'customer' is not particularly helpful. Another example also illustrates this point: within the criminal justice service 'when trying to determine who the customer is for a magistrate's court, is the customer the home office, the probation service, the police, the public or the individual citizen?' (Clark 1992: 374). Some services are designed to meet the need of the 'public' rather than any particular individual. This is so for planning permission where, for example, the siting of a hostel for homeless people could be opposed by residents yet important for the users of the hostel and society as a whole. In these situations the provider needs to make a decision on behalf of the 'collective' rather than individuals, which may give an outcome unlikely to be popular with local people. The importance here is to achieve balance between individual choice and collective need. This is where the concept of citizen widens, moving from a narrow view of the citizen with individual choice, to that of an individual viewed as a member of a community. Here 'citizens are seen as having mean-ingful existence only in the context of social networks bound together by the ties of membership, loyalty and mutual obligation . . . the activity which defines the citizen is *participation in collective purposes* rather than choice in individual purposes' (Prior, Stewart and Walsh 1995: 17). From an equalities perspective, this definition of citizen makes sense. If one is to provide services according to need, it is important to see some groups of people as members of a community which defines their needs. For example, black and minority ethnic people will face racism because of the community they live in. They will therefore need services from housing providers and the police which recognize the discrimination they face. The racism they experience is because of their membership of a group and not because of their individual characteristics (see Chapter 2).

The view that users of services should be seen as full citizens recognizes that people have a wider set of rights than if they are viewed only as customers. Moreover, it offers a wider definition than one of 'citizens as customers in a market'. Citizens, under this wide definition, have general rights to services such as education, health and justice. This does not mean that people necess-arily have rights to particular types of education, particular treatment or particular forms of redress. Such rights lend themselves to be extended to cover equal opportunities. Citizens must be seen not just to have formal rights (the right to education) but also to have substantive rights (the ability to access the education system as much as anyone else). York City Council was the first to see its users as citizens in this sense when in the 1980s it published the first 'Citizen's Charter'. This included the following rights: 'the right to know, the right to be heard, to influence, to be treated honestly, fairly and courteously, the right to participate and be represented'. This represented a seed of change in local government policy in which people were not just recognized as individuals with consumer rights but also as members of a community with rights of access to the decision-making process itself. 'Citizenship is thus a concept both of *being* and *doing*' (Prior, Stewart and Walsh 1995: 5).

It is becoming clear that there are different types of rights, all of which need to be incorporated into the concept of citizenship. Consumer rights have already been mentioned. More important are 'civil rights'. These, which were recognized in the eighteenth century, are the rights which enable individuals to participate freely in the life of the community and include rights such as freedom of speech, religion, the ownership of property and the right to justice. Added to these citizens acquired 'political rights' which are the rights to participate in the government of the community. They are the right to vote given to men in the nineteenth century and to women a century later and to choose who decides on your behalf. Finally, throughout the twentieth century we have seen the rise of social rights: 'the right to share to the full in the social heritage and to live the life of a civilised being according to the standards prevailing in society' (Marshall 1950: 11). These include the right to education, health and economic welfare. A new, slightly different, set of rights has emerged in the last 30 years: the right to be heard and recognized for what you are. These are the rights of women, black and minority ethnic people, disabled people, gay men and lesbians and so on (see Blackburn 1993).

This then is the position taken in this book which addresses issues surrounding service delivery. Citizenship as defined by rights is the concept of citizenship within which this book is framed. Services offered to the public should take into account people's rights in the widest sense. People should be able to partake in service provision on an equal footing with all other service users and not have services denied to them because of discriminatory practices in the way policies are developed, resources allocated and services delivered. This means that providers must be aware of people's different needs and of the barriers in the way services are currently designed and delivered which prevent these needs being met. 'The move to responsiveness requires the organization to be willing to vary to meet varying demands from users. It also reflects a move away from simple efficiency to the more complex combination of efficiency and effectiveness' (Prior, Stewart and Walsh 1995: 45). Until recently the prevailing view was that so long as the same service was provided to all, a provider organization would not discriminate. It assumed uniform requirements: 'uniformity was never a very accurate picture of reality, but it was part of the value base of the public service, and variation of service was never planned' (ibid.) (see Chapter 2).

Overview of the book

The book starts by considering why equal opportunities in service delivery is important (Chapter 1). The chapter argues that developing equal opportunities in service delivery helps make any organization more effective, more efficient and more competitive. This introduces the links between equalities and quality. Equal opportunities also gives the organization a better image in terms of the public's perceptions. The Football Association clearly improved its image through its 'Kick out Racism' campaign. Is the way sport is run, or for that matter any organization, ultimately accountable to the public? The chapter examines accountability in the running of services. Getting services 'right' depends on the public, those to whom the organization is accountable and the organization's staff. Having a representative workforce is important: the links between discrimination at work and discrimination in the delivery of services are also covered in this chapter.

The second chapter takes a closer look at discrimination in relation to service delivery. How, for instance, does discrimination operate? The chapter argues that equal opportunities should be about groups of people (women, black and minority ethnic people . . .) and their different characteristics and not about individuals in all their variety. The similarities and differences between 'equalities' and 'diversity' are also explored. The relevance of language, the damaging effects of stereotyping and of raising other barriers to equal access are assessed. Issues of 'double discrimination', as well as the notion of hierarchies in discrimination (is one form of discrimination worse than another?), are also analysed.

The third chapter begins by examining the legal components of discrimination in service delivery. It looks at how one can counter discrimination by using legislation. The law covers some groups of people who experience discrimination but not others. Women, black and minority ethnic people and disabled people are covered by the Sex Discrimination Act, the Race Relations Act and the Disability Discrimination Act. These Acts are looked at in some detail with illustrations from legal judgements. The organization's liability is explained. For those areas not covered by legislation (age, sexuality) the book considers what rights people have and what obligations an organization has towards them. The influence of European legislation is important in the context of equalities.

The fourth chapter is concerned with what may be needed over and above legislative requirements. It is about identifying people's needs. The chapter considers why and when organizations should consult the public and how the needs of different groups of people can be measured. It explains the different methods which can be used in consultation and assesses how meaningful each can be. It also addresses how differing needs can be balanced. The chapter covers the whole range of consultation options from simple information exchange through to user participation in the design and delivery of services. It describes how the public can be actively involved in the way in which they receive services rather than merely 'subjected' to receiving them in a particular way.

The framework needed to deliver services which do not discriminate is the topic of the fifth chapter. The chapter looks at how to develop policies on equal opportunities in service delivery. Because the overall philosophy within which policies are developed is important the chapter covers the extent to which the organization's culture and values matter. Other questions looked at are what structures are needed to develop equalities work? What should a policy cover? How should it be developed and how should it be implemented?

The chapter gives examples of policies from private, public and voluntary sector organizations together with examples of successful implementation strategies.

The sixth chapter looks at ways of measuring whether an organization is discriminating or if equal opportunities policies are working. The chapter examines ways of collecting data on users. There is no point in collecting information for no purpose and the chapter describes why the data should be used to ensure equalities in service delivery. There are different ways in which data can be used to change and advance an organization. Monitoring systems and performance indicators for equalities work are assessed. There is also an analysis of examples from the Audit Commission, the Commission for Racial Equality (CRE) and other bodies which encourage good practice.

Finding out whether discrimination occurs is not the same as being able to deliver a service which is equally fair to all. The seventh chapter is about how to change the way an organization delivers its services and adapt them to meet the needs of the public. The government requires public services to be reviewed as part of its drive for Best Value, and equalities should be an essential element of Best Value. The chapter examines ways of reviewing services to ensure that they do not discriminate. This brings together elements of the three previous chapters (consultation, policies and monitoring). Equal opportunities is about change. This chapter concentrates on means of getting an organization to adapt the way it operates to be responsive to the needs of the public. Ways in which the workforce and the public can get involved in such change are an integral part of the process described in this chapter.

In any effort to change an organization problems arise. With equal opportunities as with other areas of change there is often a lot of progress in 'talking' about the issue but very little in terms of action. Reasons for this are considered in the final chapter. Problems and barriers to developing equal opportunities in service delivery are looked at as well as possible solutions for a way forward. Specific difficulties are encountered, for example, when services are contracted and subcontracted. It is important therefore to look at the whole issue of provider and purchaser split and its effect on equal opportunities. Other barriers to change are examined and these include resistance from managers, staff and the public. There are proposals to overcome these.

1

WHY EQUAL OPPORTUNITIES IN SERVICE DELIVERY?

This chapter looks at the reasons why organizations should develop and implement policies in equal opportunities for service delivery. Managers involved in service delivery often see equal opportunities as irrelevant to their interests. This view, however, is damaging to the organization as it will inevitably prevent it from maximizing its potential. By incorporating equal opportunities principles an organization should be able to reach a wider public, respond to varied needs and offer satisfaction to a more diverse group of customers. It should be able to get closer to all potential customers rather than just its traditional clients. Failure to recognize this aspect of equal opportunities seems to arise because many managers have a narrow view of equal opportunities, seeing it as only about recruitment and selection or about providing the same service to all. Some see equal opportunities as limiting potential and about reverse discrimination in which preferential treatment is given to certain groups of people. This is not the case and in fact is against the law (see Chapter 3). Others view equalities as simply about *training* staff on race, gender or disability. Training without taking other measures does not address the discrimination which may be built into the structures and procedures of an organization. Together these views have led people to take approaches to equal opportunities work which pay lip service to equalities and which have not been effective. Equalities is about actual change in the organization.

This chapter aims to describe exactly why equalities work is of value. First it returns to a theme raised in the Introduction that customers should be viewed as citizens who have rights, and these include the right to services for different groups of people (such as black and minority ethnic people, disabled people). The chapter then goes on to address accountability. If customers have rights, questions arise: to whom are managers accountable? To the public or to the organization? Equally, to whom is the organization accountable? The chapter then looks at how an organization which takes equal opportunities seriously will be more efficient. The argument developed will be that a measure of efficiency is providing services in ways which meet people's needs and wants.

An organization that provides good quality services to everyone is likely to be more successful than one that provides for a restricted group of people. Next, the chapter explores the links between equality and quality. The relationship between equal opportunities in employment and in service delivery is also looked at, particularly in terms of increased effective delivery of services to disadvantaged groups. Finally, the chapter reviews the evidence that equal opportunities in service delivery makes good business sense.

Services should be accessible to all

Ensuring that services are accessible to all is fundamentally an ethical issue. It is about fairness. In a just society services should be available and accessible to all who want or need to use them. This principle does not preclude services being unavailable because of an organization's financial constraints. What is provided should not discriminate against any one particular group of people. This follows the principle that customers should be seen as citizens with rights. Until recently there was no concept of 'right' to a service in this sense. Certain groups of people were denied services without any intention of wrongdoing: sports sessions were largely designed to attract men and young people with few, if any, being made accessible to women and older people. Many services discriminate against certain groups, although increasingly there is an awareness that this is somehow morally wrong. For example, much of our public transport system discriminates against people with mobility disabilities. Wheelchair users still cannot easily get on a train or a bus. However, it is now widely recognized that disabled people have the same right to transport as anyone else.

In some instances ensuring that all groups of people have access to the service may sometimes mean that it is necessary to limit the use of the service by some groups to enable the service to be used by others (if resources are limited). This needs to be done if everyone is to have a fair share of the service. For example, fewer books in English could be bought for a library if this meant that books in other community languages could then be bought. However, some managers resent this access: 'I could fill this place every night with football. We only let the roller hockey team in on the condition that they set up a junior club. That's now so popular they can't understand why they can't have additional bookings. The answer is there would be no space left for women's events or the pensioners!' (quoted in LGMB 1991: 6). Moral rights to services such as sport are additional to statutory rights which organizations provide such as the right to education or the right to appeal against a planning application. Some organizations have widened the rights customers have by setting out defined rights for their customers through 'charters' or similar documents. For example Birmingham City Council has a statement of rights for residents in older people's homes. In general, the public's right of access to a service is increasingly being recognized by the private sector. British Gas has talking bills and services for deaf people and has a special 'commitment' to older and disabled customers. A recognition of these rights of access is central to the notion of citizenship. The following quote refers to local authorities but

could apply equally to any organization: 'a concern to eliminate discrimination, which is one of the most powerful barriers to substantive citizenship,
and to create a climate in which all citizens have the opportunity to pursue
their interests and fulfil their aspirations, should be central to the policies of all
local authorities. Such a strategy can be implemented in many ways, not least
by the adoption of equal opportunities practices within the authority's own
operations both as employer and as service provider' (Prior, Stewart and Walsh
1995: 159).

Accountability and equal opportunities

Public organizations, such as local authorities, are directly accountable to their
customers – the public who elect them. Quasi-public services run by appointed
bodies such as health authorities or 'quangos' (quasi non-governmental organizations) like the Training and Enterprise Councils (TECs) are indirectly accountable to their customers through the relevant Secretary of State. Private
organizations are accountable to a board of directors and their shareholders.
Consequently, accountability will mean different things to different types of
organization:

> Different service suppliers pose different problems . . . They have different
> chains of accountability: public services to elected political representa-
> tives; commercial organizations, to boards and shareholders; and not-for-
> profit agencies to management committees and trustees. Each is subject to
> different tensions. In commercial services, it's between meeting need and
> making a profit; in public provision, between meeting the needs of service
> providers and service users and in not-for-profit organizations, between
> what's needed and what will get funded.
>
> (Beresford and Croft 1993: 196)

What bearing does this have on equal opportunities? Accountability to the
customer is clearer in the case of the public sector. If the public don't like the
service they get, they can vote the administration out. For the private sector
accountability rests more on the organization's public mission statement on
what it will do for its customers than on its duty to be accountable *per se*. The
only way customers can make themselves 'count' is by removing their custom
or by buying shares in the company and removing the directors! The growth of
'charters' increases accountability through information. Knowing what an
organization promises to deliver provides a means of holding that organization to account. As a former minister, William Waldegrave said in reference
to citizen's charters, 'the government has, in fact, broken new ground in
strengthening accountability . . . knowledge is power' (quoted by Prior,
Stewart and Walsh 1995: 25). Using charters a customer can get redress
through complaints systems, the courts, the ombudsman or tribunals.

Full accountability in the public sector should mean that those who exercise
power over service users have to account for their policies (their aims and
objectives) in terms of service delivery. It means that representatives who
make decisions on behalf of the public will be held to account by those on

whose behalf they act. This is different from the process of delivery where accountability is the same as for the private sector, dependent on how the service is delivered compared with what delivery is expected from the provider, where one can complain if the service is not what is promised but where one is not involved in deciding what should be promised. For example, although the public may be involved in deciding whether an organization would have a policy on racial harassment, they are unlikely to be involved in any decision on how the policy is implemented: 'Accountability for policy differs from accountability for process in that the latter does not necessarily require the involvement of the citizen; it can be enforced by the courts, ombudsmen or audit bodies' (Prior, Stewart and Walsh 1995: 64). Accountability for policy requires the involvement of the public in a stronger sense than individuals choosing one service provider as opposed to another or challenging the quality of the service they receive.

Full accountability in terms of policies on equalities and service delivery must involve customers in the decision-making process. This will require a measure of consultation and even participation from the public (see Chapter 4 for more detail). The more informed the decision makers can be about the needs and aspirations of the public, the more accountable they will be to their service users. As more people participate in this debate, so the more will 'count'. Being accountable is about making sure that everyone 'counts' in the decisions that are made. This means that *all* people count, regardless of their gender, race, disability, age or sexuality. This will mean tackling differing, even contrasting, views and resolving them through consultation and debate with the public. In this way Prior, Stewart and Walsh talk of a society 'in which contrasting ends and purposes are resolved in collective decision. This approach involves a recognition of difference' (1995: 3). The more different the groups of people involved in decisions affecting services, the more people will feel valued as customers and take an interest in the organization, and the stronger accountability will be. Involving customers in decision making for accountability has all the problems described in the Introduction which are linked to their use of the term 'customer'. Are the police accountable to Parliament, the Home Office, the local police authority, the public, or the law itself? Most of these could count as 'customers'. Accountability will therefore be limited in clarity by the limitations of the term 'customer' itself. One of the limits in terms of accountability for unelected bodies (public and private sector) is that there are no mechanisms built into the organization for accountability of the decision-making process and no legal requirement to make any such mechanism known. There is recourse to the courts or ombudsman but this has little direct influence on policy making. Often, there is little information available to the public on how decisions are made and how they can be influenced by the public.

Effective services and equal opportunities

Being accountable improves the effectiveness of a service in as much as it ensures that services provided are those people need and want. Equal opportunities is about ensuring that services meet the needs of those groups of people who have traditionally faced disadvantage and discrimination such as women, black and minority ethnic people, disabled people, older people and lesbians and gay men. Providing services that meet people's needs is bound to be more effective than providing services that fail for certain groups of people. If the doors into a shop are too heavy or too awkward for disabled people and for older people, they are unlikely to use the shop. If a service is effective, customers are more likely to be satisfied with the service they get. Echoing this point the Commission for Racial Equality (CRE) comments: 'Delivering the services that local people need, in the most appropriate way, will increase service users' satisfaction. A good equality of opportunity policy will ensure that managers seek accurate and unbiased information about their existing and potential customers, and lead to appropriate marketing and provision of services' (CRE 1995f: 15). A guide to further education emphasizes the need to have information about customers and potential customers and to meet the 'various learning needs of men and women from all racial groups' (Commission for Racial Equality and Equal Opportunities Commission 1996: 10). The guide goes on to say, 'close and full involvement in the college of men and women from all ethnic groups will help strengthen and deepen its roots in the local community.' This will, of course, be an additional reason for pursuing equalities – the perception of the community. The guide continues, 'Further education colleges that understand and meet the needs of students from all ethnic groups, and both sexes, will be more successful in recruiting and retaining students' (CRE and EOC 1996: 10). Sylvie Pearce, whilst Chief Executive of Reading Council, also took the view that developing services to meet the needs of different groups of people is likely to be a successful strategy: 'Not equal services but highly sensitive and developed services, is a risk worth taking' (Pearce 1995: 8).

Ultimately, organizations that recognize difference and diversity among their customers will be strengthened. In the health service it is now recognized that ill health is linked to discrimination (see Chapter 2), and that by developing equal opportunities a more effective service will result. Bywaters and McLeod (1996) reported how health outcomes improved once equal opportunities principles were applied. In their example the aim was to improve older people's health by encouraging appropriate self-referral. To achieve this the project concentrated on improving information to older people by designing leaflets in large print, making them available in languages other than English and providing information on tape. The information also had an expressed commitment to the needs of lesbians and gay men. In addition, older people committed to hospital were told of the project by hospital social workers. Carers of older people with severe degrees of cognitive impairment were also briefed. The outcome was a substantial increase in the rate of self-referral (1996: 52ff.).

Quality and equality

For service delivery in general, quality has been defined as including 'knowing the customer', 'providing responsiveness, access, security, credibility, courtesy, good communication and competence' (Clark 1992: 375). Equality is about the quality of services, indeed there cannot be high-quality services without equality. Services that do not meet the needs of diverse customers will not be high-quality services. Quality for local authorities has been defined as 'providing services that match the policy commitments of the authority and meet the needs of the service user and community economically, efficiently, effectively and equitably' (LGMB 1992: 5). Linking other strategies for change to equalities is more likely to be successful. Accordingly the greater the number of managers who understand and support equal opportunities the greater the likelihood of success: 'Top management backing can be affected by the persuasiveness of change agents (whether external advisers or managers from inside) and their ability to put the case for an equality strategy which enhances, rather than conflicts with, either a business ethos or other organizational objectives (for example commissioning social services)' (Blakemore and Drake 1996: 195).

Not only is a high-quality service one in which a service is related to need or want, it is also a service where people know what they can expect. At one level, quality is about providing information (as is found in many of the charters). This information will enable customers to assess the quality of the service for themselves and choose between service providers. Where there is no choice 'information should enable people to be sure of what they will get and to plan their lives accordingly, i.e. it should empower people to make *other* choices' (Prior, Stewart and Walsh 1995: 151). Because people's needs change, information should include how the service could change in response to varying needs. 'The overall principle is that equitable quality services must be relevant and responsive services. The challenge is to create services relevant and close to the public and capable of providing a flexible response to the public in all their diversity of need and requirements' (London Borough of Haringey 1991: 4). But for best effect information to the customer must be mirrored by information from the customer. This is the way a provider can identify changing needs. People's needs vary and for services to be responsive to need, mechanisms must be in place to provide information about customers' changing needs. Clearly, organizations with strategies which allow for flexibility and change will be more effective, close to, and responsive to their customers and will also empower staff at all levels to respond to change. It can also mean empowering customers to participate in the specifications of the service itself. In this way users will have a stake in the service which in itself will increase accountability, and will be more likely to see the service as relevant to their needs.

It is not enough to look at the links between quality and equality. It is also important to address the differences between a quality approach and an equalities approach. The following example, from my own experience, illustrates how a top quality service with a good customer care approach can fail to deliver on equalities. During my time as a councillor in Hammersmith and Fulham, I was told about the excellent service provided for children who could not afford to go on holiday. The council organized a summer camp in the New Forest for children from the poorest estates. Families from these estates were given the opportunity of a holiday with their children on a camp site specially set up by the council each year. I was told how successful these summer camps were, with the staff working closely with the customers. Customers came back year after year and gave glowing reports of their time in these holiday camps. I was invited to go down to the New Forest, help set the camp up and watch the customers arrive in their coaches. The first coaches to arrive came from estates I knew well where up to 50 per cent of residents were black. To my amazement all the families coming off the coaches were white. Highly satisfied customers indeed, but a highly discriminatory service. The staff were also almost entirely white and when questioned had not realized how few of their customers were black. A similar experience was also happening in another part of the Play Service in that borough: the under-5s service. Here again was a service which seemed almost entirely 'white', staff and users alike, even in areas where a large proportion of the population was black. Again very loyal, highly satisfied customers but a discriminatory service. These examples illustrate that good quality and customer care are not the same as ensuring equalities in service delivery.

One crucial aspect of 'quality' is customer care. It is important to consider how customer care relates to equalities. Customer care is being responsive to customer needs, being close to the customer, finding out the public's view, ensuring good information on services and developing good staff–public relationship. To be truly effective, customer care should adopt an equalities perspective and embrace all aspects of equalities, but equally it can fail to do so as in the example of the summer camp organized by Hammersmith and Fulham. You can have what appears to be a high-quality service with full user participation and yet fail to provide an equitable service. Problems arise when the service is discriminatory and all its users are from one group. These users may be highly satisfied with the service they receive, but others may feel differently. For example, the sports centre which provides a service almost entirely for men may be very responsive to its customer needs, have an excellent relationship between staff and customer, provide value for money and yet (since it does not cater for the needs of women) it cannot be seen as a good quality service from an equalities perspective. The problem is that for many of those involved in providing a service, customer means 'actual customer' whereas for equalities to be ensured it must also mean 'potential customer'. As the LGMB made clear in terms of local government: 'The links between service quality and equality have still to be made. The specific experiences and power position of groups of customers – whether these are defined in terms of gender, ethnic origin, sexuality, age, physical ability or other criteria – are often ignored. Service quality means ensuring that all groups of customers are able to gain access to and receive equal treatment from the local authority' (LGMB 1991: 17–18).

Quality covers areas of management practice which provide high-quality services such as availability, standards, timeliness, speed and reliability. It also includes staff attributes such as courtesy, responsiveness, competence, communication, security and credibility. Quality also pertains to the environment: access, appearance and locality. And finally quality is linked to the customer itself in terms of choice, rights, information and redress. (This list is drawn from 'Customer criteria for judging service quality' LGMB 1991: 16). There is a fuller discussion on quality and equality in Chapter 6. To achieve all this it is necessary to have good management systems, to involve staff and to involve users. Most of these quality elements also have an 'equalities' dimension which if ignored will mean an organization fails to achieve high-quality standards. In 1991 Haringey Council produced a list of an Equality/Quality Assurance System for Council Services which is as follows:

The key characteristics of Equitable Quality Services are that they will provide all the people of Haringey's various communities with services that:-

1 *Are relevant* – To achieve this,
  - A range of different types of services will be offered as appropriate.
  - Gaps/changes/developments in Services will be actively identified.
  - Service priorities will be regularly assessed and resources allocated to meet relevant needs.
  - The equalities dimension of service delivery will be monitored and the analysis of results used to inform future Service planning.
  - Information on the nature of the Service will be available in a variety of easily accessible ways, including community languages.
  - Surveys and other methods will be used to identify needs and experiences of users and 'front line' staff.
  - Member level local fora will be set up to enable the participation of an informed public and local users in Service developments.

2 *Are accessible* – To achieve this,
  - Services will be available from locations that are accessible by public transport, and have access for people with disabilities. It will be made clear how to complain and what to expect.

3 *Are caring* – To achieve this,
  - Services will be provided in a caring and sensitive manner.
  - Complaints will be dealt with quickly and complainants informed of the action taken and redress offered.
  - Public areas of offices will provide proper facilities for callers.
  - Telephone messages will be responded to quickly.

(London Borough of Haringey 1991: 5)

Equal opportunities is a majority issue

Equal opportunities is important in as much as it concerns the majority of people in the population. The 1991 census gives the following figures:

- 52 per cent of the population are women and this is even across the country.
- 5.5 per cent of the population are from black or minority ethnic groups. This rises to 20 per cent in Greater London where 45 per cent of minority ethnic people live. Within London there are great variations from borough to borough with Brent having 45 per cent of the population black and minority ethnic and Richmond 6 per cent. Within this, of course, there are also variations for different ethnic groups, with some areas having mainly Caribbean people (Hackney) and others mainly Asian (Tower Hamlets).

Approximately half the minority ethnic population in the UK is Asian with Indians comprising the largest group. Of black and minority ethnic people 80 per cent are under 25. Minority ethnic communities have a higher proportion of people at university and are better qualified compared to the white population, yet are twice as likely to be unemployed (see CRE 1995d).

- Disability was not recorded in the 1991 census. However, it is estimated that there are 6.5 million disabled people in the UK (just over 11 per cent) of whom one million are blind or partially sighted (Massie 1994: 8). Two-thirds of disabled people are older people (over 60 years old) and just over a quarter million of disabled people are under 25. Approximately two million disabled people are of working age and 70 per cent of these are unemployed. Those that are employed tend to earn considerably less than non-disabled people (see Massie 1994: 25). One in four households has at least one disabled member.

- People over 65 account for approximately 16 per cent of the population. Of these most are white. Among black and minority ethnic people 3.2 per cent are over 65. The fastest rate of increase in the minority ethnic population is within this age group (see CRE 1995a: 4). Contrary to the white population where most older people are women, the majority of minority ethnic elders are men. There are differences between minority ethnic groups with, for example, Bangladeshi men outnumbering women by a much larger margin than that found among other minority ethnic groups.

- Lesbians and gay men also did not figure in the census. Estimates suggest that 10 per cent of the population are lesbians or gay men. This figure rises in London and is generally higher in cities where there is a more liberal environment and more facilities for lesbians and gay men.

All these different groups have different needs and may require different services. Taken together and allowing for overlaps, these groups account for nearly 70 per cent of the population. You simply add to 52 per cent minority ethnic males (e.g. add 2.7 per cent), white men over 65 (approximately 6 or 7 per cent), white disabled men under 65 and white able-bodied gay men under 65 to produce the final figure. This quite clearly means that equal opportunities is not, as is often believed, a 'minority issue' but on the contrary it is a 'majority issue' and therefore central to day-to-day service delivery.

Employment and service delivery

There are links between equal opportunities in employment and in service delivery. A workforce representative of the community the organization serves is more likely to be able to deliver services according to need simply because there would be a greater understanding of various needs by a workforce whose members also shared those needs. If the predominant culture of an organization is white and male, the few women within the organization will have difficulty getting their voices heard, so, 'For example, women managers in male-dominated environments may not always be heard in meetings because of men's shared views about women's roles' (LGMB 1991: 35). If the culture of an organization makes employees feel ignored, isolated, marginalized and undervalued, it will inevitably affect the service delivery to customers. Additionally, if these members of staff are also residents in the locality, word will spread through the community that the organization is unfriendly to certain groups of people (black and minority ethnic people, women, disabled people, lesbians and gay men or older people), whereas on the other hand, 'Full involvement in the organization of men and women from diverse ethnic groups will help strengthen and deepen local roots' (CRE, EOC and CVCP 1997: 4). Thus the culture of an organization can determine the context in which decisions are made and therefore impacts on service delivery: 'Because organizational policy-making and service design decisions tend to be made by one group, there will be a propensity for their values, beliefs and perceptions to predominate. These perceptions will include stereotypes about other groups' (LGMB 1991: 83). Having a diverse workforce with staff from different backgrounds and cultures should create a workforce with more ideas and flexibility of mind. This in turn means that change is easier. Ross and Schneider (1992) see this as part of the 'business case' for a diverse workforce. An organization with a representative workforce is more able to anticipate customers' changing needs and thus create a more effective service delivery. The same point is made by the CRE in relation to ethnicity: 'A local authority workforce that reflects the ethnic diversity of its community will help to ensure a responsive and appropriate service for service users' (1995f: 15). The CRE develops the same argument in *Racial Equality Means Business*: 'a diverse workforce can help the organization to plan more successful marketing or service delivery strategy' (1995e). See also the EOC report, *'Equal Opportunity Makes Good Business Sense'* (1991), which also links equal opportunities in employment with good service delivery. Different groups of staff bring with them different experiences, different cultures and languages, different knowledge (of gender, ethnicity, disability, sexuality, age) which can all be harnessed by the organization: 'Although these benefits include increased profitability, they go beyond financial measures to encompass learning, creativity, flexibility, organizational and individual growth, and the ability of a company to adjust rapidly and successfully to market changes' (Thomas and Ely 1996: 80). Customers will be more likely to feel that they are being treated equally if the staff serving them include people who are similar to themselves. A black customer will not feel as confident if all staff are white.

Good employment practices in terms of equal opportunities need to include more than a representative workforce it they are going to have an impact on service delivery. They also need to include a workforce that itself is not experiencing discrimination. That is to say that in addition to policies on recruitment and selection, they need to have policies on promotion, training, redundancy and harassment. If an organization had harassment procedures which applied to customers but not to staff, it would be unlikely that these procedures will be enthusiastically endorsed by the staff. A local authority which had a clear procedure for racial harassment in relation to customers (say on a housing estate where racial attacks had occurred) yet allowed its black staff to be subjected to racial harassment from other members of staff, without recourse to redress, would not be successful in trying to get its staff to

implement its racial harassment procedures for its customers. Treating everyone fairly should also lead to retention of trained committed staff.

The business case for equal opportunities in service delivery

It is widely accepted that equal opportunities makes good business sense.
British Gas, together with several disability organizations, has published a
leaflet called *Good Practice, Great Business* (1997) in which it outlines what it
does for disabled customers. The leaflet also reminds readers: 'Disabled people,
their family and friends, control a significant amount of the country's income.
These customers have a choice, you must serve the customer or die' (a quote
from Sainsbury's). As a corollary to this a disabled customer is quoted as
saying: 'When I find somewhere that is accessible I stick with it – they get my
custom again and again. Equally, the attitudes of staff count for a lot.' For
example, it is estimated that the minority ethnic community has a disposable
income of £10 billion a year and this section of the population will double over
the next few years (see *Equalities News* 1997: 8). 'Race for Opportunity' is a
campaign which aims to encourage businesses to invest in minority ethnic
communities, arguing that minority ethnic communities offer a growing
customer base. Goods and services could be marketed more actively and more
effectively to these communities. Examples of businesses which have joined
'Race for Opportunity' include the Bank of England, the BBC, Boots the
Chemist, Littlewoods, WH Smith, the TSB, Midland Bank, British Airways
and Northern Foods plc. The TSB undertook a major survey in the West
Midlands to 'identify perceptions and understandings of the business by
ethnic minority customers'. Fox Biscuits, produced by Northern Foods plc,
developed a biscuit specially for the Muslim community in West Yorkshire.
The biscuits are without animal fat and therefore do not contain pork
products. A company able to attract customers with different needs will
broaden its customer base and gain competitive advantage. Marks and Spencer
understands this well. It has a large sign, prominently displayed outside most
of its shops, which reads, 'We are happy to help. Please ask our staff for
assistance'. With this invitation are signs for wheelchair users, people who
are visually impaired and people who are hearing impaired. Other retail shops
like Tesco offer help in a variety of ways to disabled customers – one example is
special trolleys which do not require the user to bend down or which fit onto a
wheelchair. Many supermarkets also cater for minority ethnic customers and
have specialist foods publicized in different languages (for example Greek and
Turkish food in Islington supermarkets).

   All service provision benefits from equal opportunities policies. Outside
building sites in the London Borough of Richmond, a large sign from the
council says: 'The Contractor on this project is a member of the London
Borough of Richmond upon Thames' Considerate Contractor Scheme and
has agreed to abide by the following Code of Good Practice.' The code then
includes a paragraph which reads: 'All work will be carried out safely and in
such a way that it will not inconvenience pedestrians or road users. Special
care will be taken to make sure that pedestrians with sight, hearing or mobility

difficulties are not inconvenienced or endangered and that access is maintained for those in wheelchairs or pushing prams.' I would rather be a resident in such a borough than any other if I had a disability or small children. These initiatives also help build trust and even loyalty between customers and organizations. This is particularly true for groups of people who have traditionally been excluded from access to many services or received poor service compared with other customers (for example disabled people or older people at a supermarket which only had huge, heavy trolleys).

Another business advantage gained by equal opportunities in service delivery is the creation of a good public image. Those retailers who do provide facilities for different groups of people and those who publicly declare themselves as providing services for all groups of people will project a more caring image to the public. An example of the importance of this is the Football Association's efforts to eradicate racism within the game. There was a time when football was notorious as a racist game. Racist taunts of black players by white audiences were so common that black spectators did not feel at ease in the stadiums. Only 2 per cent of supporters attending matches are black and although 25 per cent of professional footballers are black there was in 1997 only one black manager. Racism loses customers to the game but also gives the game a poor public image. In 1992 the Football Association decided to take action and launched its 'Let's Kick Racism Out of Sport' campaign, in conjunction with the Commission for Racial Equality, the Professional Footballers' Association and the Football Trust. 'Kick Out Racism' 'aims to cover all sections of the football world and involve all major football organizations' (CRE 1995c). Announcements are now regularly made at most grounds warning that racist chanting and behaviour will not be tolerated. Football clubs also warn members that they will be expelled for racist behaviour (see CRE 1996b). Sponsored by Midland Bank, a play on racism, *Kicking It Out*, opened in 1994, toured schools around the country and had a performance in the House of Commons (see Figure 1). Dave Hill in *Out of his Skin: the John Barnes Phenomenon* emphasizes that racist abuse is not a joke: 'it is not the words that matter, it is what those words mean. Racial abuse, at this point in British history . . . strips a man or woman of their identity, goads their exclusion from the right to equal treatment, their right to be an individual, their right to dignity. It attacks that man or woman's status as a human being' (quoted by the CRE 1995c: 8). Other sports are now following suit. The Rugby League started to take action in 1996 and has launched a 13-point action plan to tackle racism in rugby league. There is also a campaign in cricket called 'Hit Racism for Six' (for these examples, see CRE 1996d: 11). In these examples about sport, taking equal opportunities in terms of race seriously will mean a better service in terms of sporting events and a wider customer base attending such events. The same will be true for the image of any organization which makes it publicly known that it takes equal opportunities issues seriously and is doing something about it. Advice for further education establishments also mentions the fact that a good public image on equalities is likely to attract partnerships with other agencies: 'A further education college that is respected by all in the community will attract partnerships from a variety of agencies, such as local authorities, Training and Enterprise Councils and private sector employers' (CRE and EOC

Figure 1   Give Racism the Red Card. Winner of the Midland Bank 'Kicking Racism Out of Football' Competition, Verity Worthington, age 12.

1996: 10). A recent example of good public image associated with disability is that of British Telecom which advertised in the national papers in May 1997 with a picture of the athlete Peter Hull, winner of three Paralympic gold medals, and a caption which says, 'Don't look at the disability. Look at the ability.' BT sponsors disability swimming in the UK and funds regional and national championships. Another example is Harrington Brewery which supports the annual gay festival 'Pride'.

A final reason for believing that equal opportunities makes business sense is that discrimination, if found, could cost money as a result of litigation. This is true for ethnicity, gender and disability where the Race Relations Act, the Sex Discrimination Act and the Disability Discrimination Act have sections which make organizations liable if they discriminate against actual or potential customers (see Chapter 3 for details of these Acts). As the guide on further education warns, 'discrimination is expensive; it costs money, undermines staff morale and reputation, and makes the college unattractive to students' (CRE and EOC 1996: 10). Adverse publicity from cases or even from a formal investigation, which the CRE and the EOC are empowered to carry out in suspected discrimination by organizations, are additional expensive liabilities. This legal cost is in addition to the cost of losing customers. Racism in schools is often blamed for the fact that many more black children end up excluded from schools than white children. This has huge cost implications: 'The cost of educating an excluded pupil is about twice the cost of a standard classroom education; in 1994/5 the figures for each secondary pupil were £4,300 against £2,815. The final bill is even higher when health, social services, police and criminal justice costs are taken into account' (CRE 1996d: 10).

Conclusion

This chapter has looked at various arguments for developing equal oppor-tunities policies in service delivery. Some are to do with equity and fairness, others with efficiency and cost. The CRE makes the business case for racial equality, saying that this entails 'using people's talents to the full . . ., ensur-ing that selection decisions and policies are based on objective criteria, and not on unlawful discrimination, prejudice or unfair assumption . . ., becoming an 'employer of choice' . . ., getting closer to customers and understanding their needs . . ., operating internationally with success . . ., sustaining a healthy society . . ., making the company more attractive to investors . . ., making the company more attractive to customer and clients . . ., avoiding the costs of discrimination' (quoted in *Equal Opportunities Review* 1995: 17). An organiz-ation should always ask itself, 'what is the cost of not doing anything?' The cost of *not* having clear, implemented policies on equal opportunities can be very high: it can lead to a poor public image, the inability to retain customers, the inability to change, adapt and be flexible enough to attract new customers, and for some services and some groups of customers the cost of litigation. But what exactly is equal opportunities about? We have referred so far to the importance of diversity and to the detrimental effects of discrimination. But what exactly do these terms mean? Which groups of people face discrimi-nation and why? This is the topic of the next chapter.

2

HOW SERVICES CAN
DISCRIMINATE

The aim of this chapter is to show how discrimination operates. The chapter will argue that discrimination is about groups and their characteristics and not about individual characteristics: someone experiences discrimination because they belong to a particular group. Group differences are at the root of discriminatory practices. For example, women are different from men and different ethnic groups have different characteristics. Discrimination arises either because difference is ignored and therefore people's needs are not met, or because difference is recognized but forms the basis of unfavourable treatment, or because difference is recognized but fixed into a stereotypical view that does not equate with reality and therefore means that genuine differences are not being taken into account. Different groups have different needs according to their different characteristics. That discrimination occurs if someone is treated less favourably because of their difference is straightforward. This chapter will therefore concentrate on examining the way in which treating everyone the same can discriminate. This also includes an analysis of the nature of discrimination and the manner in which stereotypical recognition of difference can lead to discrimination. This analysis will include discussion of the way words can be used to stereotype groups of people and language can therefore be used to discriminate. Finally the chapter argues for the need to recognize genuine differences and give an account of the different needs of different groups, looking at the way discrimination operates against each group. Issues such as 'double discrimination', where someone may be experiencing discrimination on grounds of their gender as well as their ethnicity, and 'hierarchies of oppression' in which certain groups of people experience more discrimination than others, are also covered.

Difference matters

An important aspect of equal opportunities is that it is not about providing the same service to all – the so called 'colour blind' or 'gender blind' approach –

but it is about providing services which are sensitive to difference. Equal opportunities in service delivery is about providing different services according to need. Quite commonly one hears, 'we don't discriminate here, we provide exactly the same service to everyone regardless of race, disability . . .'. Traditionally public services were designed to be uniform, the aim was for 'uniformity and standardisation, so that much the same service would be available to everyone' (Prior, Stewart and Walsh 1995: 14). Providing exactly the same service to everyone is discriminatory since it ignores difference and cannot match the needs of different groups of people; some will therefore lose out and not be able to get access to the service. Anne Phillips makes this point in *Democracy and Difference* where she says: 'As long as people have different needs or capacities, then the kind of equality that meters out exactly the same to each of us in turn will effectively mean inequality: the abstract measuring volume of equal rights is insensitive to varying need' (1993: 44). 'Same service' to all quite often means a service designed by those in 'power' and this can frequently mean a service which meets the needs of white able-bodied men, simply because they fail to recognize needs that are different from their own and tend to be in decision-making positions.

One example which illustrates this well is the design of public toilets. When I was a councillor in the London Borough of Hammersmith and Fulham, an elderly woman recounted the following story. She had been shopping in Shepherd's Bush and had several full shopping bags when she felt the need to go to the toilet. Shepherd's Bush Green is a green in West London surrounded by a very busy roundabout. She waited for the traffic to come to a stop, crossed the road onto the green and went into a 'super loo'. Inside, she put down her bags and her walking sticks and took some time preparing herself to sit down. Just when she was installed on the loo the doors opened onto the rush hour traffic. Everyone turned to stare as she sat there not knowing what to do next. In the event she drew up her knickers in as dignified a manner as she could. Toilet doors open automatically to ensure that the homeless do not take up residence. As it happens the timing for this super loo had been calculated by an engineer. He was probably not elderly and not disabled and may even have forgotten that some people sit down to pee! This is an example of a service designed to suit all equally but failing to meet the needs of older people and disabled people (a significant proportion of the population).

Street lighting provides another illustration of needs that differ. In the 1980s, various surveys were conducted by local government 'Women's Units' on street lighting. The odd thing was (and still largely is) that street lighting is designed according to rules agreed by engineers over the years. These rules require that lights light the roads (not the pavements) and that the strength of the light depends on the number of cars going down the road. In my innocence as a councillor, I assumed lights were for pedestrians and their safety. When I asked the engineers they assured me that the safety of cars was more important. Then I realized that these were men who rarely walked anywhere, but drove everywhere. They had unwittingly, over the years, designed the system to suit themselves. Surveys undertaken at the time (notably by the GLC) showed that women felt very strongly that they would prefer the pavements lit and better lighting in the small roads where there wasn't much traffic. Perhaps it should come as no surprise that most drivers are men and most pedestrians are women. Black and minority ethnic people, disabled people and older people are also more likely to be pedestrians. Street lighting, like so much else in the eighties, was shown to be an equalities issue. Both of these histories give examples of services designed by one group of people for the benefit of all. People believed at the time that the service was for all and that needs were uniform across the population: 'when equality is theorised through concepts which simply presume we are the same, then it can end up favouring those who most fit, and forcing all others into a singular mould' (Phillips 1993: 48).

Quite commonly service providers see the public as essentially 'male', with anyone else some kind of deviation from the norm. Thus, for example, public meetings traditionally were designed to attract men (as if all the public were all male) and held in the evenings when most women are busy at home. When women were taken into account they were expected to adapt to male norms: when sports centres tried to offer 'women's activities', they still expected women to go down dark alleyways, have male coaches, and not have any caring responsibilities. Sports centres were rarely made women-friendly and women were seen as a diversion. As Phillips says: 'when men and women are treated the same, it means women being treated as if they were men; when men and women are treated differently, the man remains the norm, against which the woman is peculiar, lacking, different' (1993: 45). Similarly it may be the case that all the services in a locality are available to all people but in reality many cannot use them if they are not geared towards their needs: 'they may be formally entitled to use a wide range of public services and resources, but be effectively prevented from doing so by barriers such as lack of transport, racial or sexual discrimination, or simply lack of knowledge about what is available' (Prior, Stewart and Walsh 1995: 11). Providing the same service to everyone will in effect mean discrimination against certain groups of people.

What is discrimination?

Discrimination occurs when someone is treated less favourably because of their difference, but more often when someone's difference and needs are not recognized. People are discriminated against on either of these grounds because of their membership of a group. Those groups which are most often seen to experience discrimination are women, black and minority ethnic people, disabled people, older people and lesbians and gay men. This list is by no means exhaustive. One could add people with a criminal record, refugees, unemployed people and people in the social class that used to be called 'working class'. This book will restrict itself to looking at the first five different groups mentioned above but the principles underlying discrimination are similar for all groups.

No one in our society lives as an individual disconnected from the rest of their community. We all have links with one community or another defined either by our neighbourhood, our social interests (e.g. allotment society or sports club), or other groups with which we identify (e.g. the disabled or gay community). All these contribute to define who we are, our individual identity: 'People do not identify themselves purely as individuals; they frequently identify themselves, and articulate their needs and interests, as members of a social group or collectivity' (Prior, Stewart and Walsh 1995: 153). People feel they belong together because of shared experience (living in the same village, shared experience of racism) or shared interests (fight to save a wood from developers, love of opera): 'The individual has existence only within a network of social relations. This is not a matter of choice: people are *constituted* as individuals through relationships of reciprocity with others' (Prior, Stewart and Walsh 1995: 169). Groups of people have certain characteristics in common and these are shared by the individuals within the group. Not only do individuals form their own sense of belonging through these relationships to others, but society as a whole judges people according to perceived group characteristics (sometimes correctly assigned to the group, sometimes not) and this is where discrimination occurs. People who are black or from a minority ethnic group which is not 'white' will be defined not just by their own individual characteristics but also by the fact that they belong to the group of people who are not perceived as 'white' and this carries with it judgements and behaviour towards them based on their membership of the group (black and minority ethnic people). This judgement results from years of assumptions and beliefs white people have about black and minority ethnic people. This is the root of racism. The same is true for all groups of people considered by this book, all groups who are excluded from society and traditionally have little share in social, economic or political power: 'It is true that we are unique individuals, but our individuality is shaped by the social context of our lives and their structuring by "race", gender, class, age and other divisions. We need individually appropriate services which take account of these social dimensions' (Carpenter 1996: 129).

Discrimination is about power

Inequalities are reinforced in employment, education and the media. Those in positions of power in society wittingly or unwittingly operate in such a way that those who do not have power remain powerless. Power is defined as the ability to act or have influence – being in positions which allow for decision making, wealth, independence. If you are male/white/able-bodied/young or heterosexual you will have power over anyone who is female/black or from a minority ethnic group/disabled/old/lesbian or gay simply by being who you are. You are, for example, more likely to have a better job, better education and be among the group that figures most in the media. It isn't that all people of one group go out of their way to gain power (although some do), they simply live in a society which accords privileges to members of those groups. These privileges are part of the way society and systems operate, so for example if you are black or from a minority ethnic group, or a single parent (most probably women) you are more likely to be offered poor quality accommodation (see LGMB 1991: 75). Abuse of power is embodied in sexism, racism, ableism, ageism and heterosexism – mechanisms for maintaining power. Power of one group over another takes two forms. The first operates through political, economic and cultural control and in this way 'institutions which have the power to reward, enable, regulate and distribute . . . are mainly managed by white, able-bodied men' (LGMB 1991: 76). The second form of power is ideological and operates by justifying discrimination. This is part of the way in which, for example, the media will portray women, black and minority ethnic people and so on as second-class citizens.

It is not uncommon for powerless groups to justify to themselves their lack of power and 'internalize' their oppression – for example disabled people accepting that they are a burden to society and do not have the right of access to buildings and transport in the same way as able-bodied people. Only in the last 20 years or so have groups started to conceptualize the situation they find themselves in. In the 1970s women used the term 'patriarchy' to describe the power men had over them. But women themselves often feel they deserve to be in the situation they find themselves in and blame themselves for it. Women who are raped are seen as asking for it, as are women who experience domestic violence. Often they are labelled mentally ill. The 'battered women syndrome' sought to show women as suffering from some kind of breakdown rather than justifiably upset at being beaten up. An example I experienced myself, whilst a councillor, concerned the way women who are unhappy or depressed by their situation are treated as mentally ill rather than justified in their despair. In Shepherd's Bush in the early 1980s a group of women on a very deprived estate formed a self-help group called WAMH (Women Action for Mental Health). These were women who had for years gone to the doctor with a variety of complaints and been prescribed anti-depressants. This group of women, through the support of a counsellor, got themselves off drugs. The result was that a group of fairly docile women who had previously accepted their lot (poor services – housing, transport, shops, play facilities and health) became angry and demanded better. One day they called for a meeting with all the doctors at the surgery and told them what they thought of the way they were treated. They organized campaigns against the council demanding better services for their estate. No doubt the authorities would have liked them to be back on tranquillizers. It is simpler for society to keep women quiet than deal with their complaints. Those in power thus attempt to maintain it through controlling other groups. Aveen Maguire describes this in relation to women in an article called 'Power: now you see it, now you don't. A women's guide to how power works'. Here she describes the case of 'Anne', a woman experiencing domestic violence who seeks help and is prescribed valium: 'Because these issues pose a threat, those with power to take a decision on them decide not to respond to the issues but instead control them so that the threat is contained . . . Anne's tension and anxiety – the symptoms of her problems – are dealt with; she is helped to "cope" with the way things are, not to change the way things are. Her personal power to create enough fuss to have her demands attended to is undermined by the help she is offered. This is power being used directly to exercise social control' (Maguire 1992: 20). Domestic violence raises awkward questions as it is about male power over women.

Power as used to control a group of people is often referred to as 'oppression'. This is defined by the Local Government Management Board as 'the one-way, systematic and institutionalised mistreatment of one group by another, by virtue of the power that the latter holds' (LGMB 1991: 75). Oppression has a connotation of weight being put upon the shoulders of one group of people, holding them down. The point is that women, black and minority ethnic people and other groups do not just 'happen' to miss out on the power white men enjoy, 'they are actively subordinated by the holders of power' (Phillips 1992: 205). Some forms of oppression are blatant: the denial of basic human rights. Others are more subtle: ensuring that rights never get fully exercised. Anne Phillips continues in the same article: 'Sexual oppression shares with racial oppression the tendency to operate on two different levels. In both cases there have been long periods of history when the oppressed were denied their very place in humanity; in both cases the successful negotiation of this major hurdle (as, for example, when women and black people are admitted to the category of those who can vote) seems to leave the structures of oppression intact' (1992: 208). Another example: disabled people were denied entry to the United States during the main period of immigration (1880s to 1920s), being seen as undesirable along with criminals and those with mental illness (see the Ellis Island Museum of Immigration, New York). Now disabled people are allowed entry to the country to the same extent as other groups of people, but discrimination within the country still exists and disabled people still *feel* treated as undesirable.

Discrimination can be direct or indirect

The legal aspect of these terms is developed in Chapter 3. *Direct discrimination* is overt and obvious to the recipient at least. Signs which used to say in pubs 'No Jews, No Blacks' (these are now outlawed by the Race Relations Act) are direct discrimination, as are those that sometimes still say 'No Travellers'. Similarly golf clubs, open to the public, which do not admit women are practising direct discrimination. This sort of discrimination is sometimes called 'personal' as it is directed at the person. In *Disabled People and Social Justice*, Bert Massie gives an example of direct discrimination on the grounds of disability: 'In 1983 there was a celebrated case in Teignmouth where a hotelier refused accommodation to people with learning difficulties on the grounds that their disabilities might upset other guests' (1994: 9). This would now be unlawful under the Disability Discrimination Act (see Chapter 3). *Indirect discrimination* occurs where conditions are such that the outcome is discriminatory even if there was no intention to discriminate. Wheelchair users are not barred from buses, but the design of most buses effectively excludes them. The way the whole transport system is organized discriminates against disabled people. On most trains in Britain, if you use a wheelchair you still have to travel in the luggage van and be chained to the sides. If information on a service is only put out in English, this is indirect discrimination against those who do not speak English. It isn't that anyone intends to discriminate, rather that the results of their actions mean that some groups cannot get access to the service. Because of the way the system works, particular groups of people lose out. Ill health is more common among black and minority ethnic groups because of indirect discrimination: 'Through our experience of health and illness, inequalities are lived out physically and psychologically: they take bodily form in our daily lives. Our bodies are a site of oppressive social relations' (Bywaters and McLeod 1996: 16).

Discrimination can make people 'invisible'

The needs of different groups of people frequently go unrecognized and the people themselves become 'invisible'. For example, statistics are kept by the police on incidents of domestic violence. Few of these statistics give a gender breakdown (how many victims are female, how many perpetrators are male). This allows the police to maintain a 'gender blind' approach and disregard the fact that domestic violence is almost always violence by men towards women (it is a form of discrimination). Ignoring this fact leads to poor service provision and such services therefore themselves become discriminatory. Even when gender breakdowns are given, a complete analysis is often lacking and the gender implication remains invisible. For example, in Croydon, the police keep a gender breakdown which shows that approximately 20 per cent of victims are male. What is not said, however, is that when these figures are broken down, most of these male victims are men being hit by men (brothers, son and father, men in gay relationships) or men being injured by women defending themselves. In very few cases are they men being hit by women partners. (This example comes from my own experience working with the police in Croydon where statistics are reported to the Police Consultative Sub-committee on domestic violence.)

Different groups of people may have equal rights of citizenship but in practice equality is often denied because difference is ignored: 'Equal citizenship is extended to people *despite* their differences of birth, education, occupation, gender or race. It is a slippery slope from saying that these differences should not count, to saying that they don't even matter . . . There is no procedure that has proved itself so well suited to disguising women's oppression as the division into public and private spheres; by directing our attention to specifically political or civil equalities, citizenship helps obscure what goes on in the home' (Phillips 1993: 77–8). In this way domestic violence was 'invisible' as a crime until relatively recently. In the example given above of street lighting the needs of all but car drivers were 'invisible'. The engineers were completely unaware of any other groups of people who might require street lighting. Examples of 'invisibility' occur when people's experiences of discrimination are denied. When a woman is raped her experiences are often not taken into account; if she says 'no' (even repeatedly) this is sometimes taken as meaning 'yes' if, for example, the 'defendant says he understood it was a cry of ecstasy' (Kennedy 1993: 129). Thus the criminal justice system discriminates against women: 'It is often the way with discriminatory practice that its victims know full well what is happening whilst those who perpetrate it are oblivious. Denying women their experience is one of the ways in which male power is maintained' (Kennedy 1993: 15). Similar examples can be given for older people, disabled people and other groups who frequently simply do not figure in the planning of services. Specific examples illustrating the discrimination different groups face will be given further on in this chapter.

Invisibility is a mark of discrimination. I once took note, in 1995, of who spoke at meetings (male, female, black or white) and compared my notes with those of a 'trained' minute taker (this was at committee meetings and other senior officer meetings of a local authority). I found that repeatedly, if the note taker was male or white, things said by women or black people were not recorded; they had become 'invisible'. This did not always occur, but over a period of several months was frequent enough to reveal a pattern. It was the same minute takers who were at fault each time. Similar experiments were done with the media in the 1970s and 1980s: 'A spot check on two national "quality" newspapers on 14 July 1986 revealed that the news pages of the *Guardian* included reports of 182 named individuals, of whom 21 were female. The *Daily Telegraph* on the same day featured 30 women among 193 named individuals' (Coote and Campbell 1987: 208). During news coverage of the 1997 general election the Fawcett Society monitored appearances by politicians. Over a week, out of 135 appearances, 8 were by women. Of 138 items presented, 28 were presented by women journalists; among professionals and business people only 4 out of 54 were women. Women who did appear on the news were members of the public being interviewed in well-defined women's roles, usually as mothers (*Equalities News* 1997: 9). When women do appear in the press it is usually from a male point of view as 'wives' or 'mums', rarely from a woman's own perspective. Who decides what is newsworthy and what is not? Women make up half the population yet become invisible in large sections of the press. An article in the *British Medical Journal* reported on the rape of women in the Gulf War and commented on how traumatic it was for the men who had to watch! No mention was made of the effect on the women (see Collier and Collier 1991). Betty Friedan repeated the work she had done in the 1960s on the media and women (published in *The Feminine Mystique*, 1963) and found that older people are equally invisible in the press: 'In *Vogue*, of 290 identifiable faces in ads, there was only *one* of a woman who might have been over sixty – in a tiny snapshot of "me and granny"' (Friedan 1994:5). All groups who face discrimination are still largely 'invisible' as members of the public. In one local authority a seminar given for all top managers used a slide presentation showing the pressures on the council. One pressure was 'the public' and the drawing showed a group of three young able-bodied men and one woman. No one saw anything wrong with it. This is the view many people in senior positions have of 'the public'.

Language can be used to discriminate

This occurs when language is used carelessly and misused. George Orwell claimed 'the slovenliness of our language makes it easier for us to have foolish thoughts' (quoted by Mair 1992: 57). Communication is about getting the right message across. Where language is used to communicate it needs to be clear, unambiguous and effective if we are to succeed in imparting information. Language is a very powerful tool: 'language is inseparable from power. It reflects inequalities and must change if they are to be challenged . . . So long as identities are devalued the terms attached to them will constantly be changing' (Beresford and Croft 1993: 84). The way we talk and write about the world can affect the way we regard and interact with other people. Indeed language can exclude people and make them appear invisible ('man-kind', 'manmade' – where are women?). It can make people feel inferior to the norm ('manageress' where the norm is 'manager'). It can be stereotypical and give a false image of one group of people ('fairy' to mean gay); patronizing ('old dear' for 'older person'); demeaning ('handicapped' for 'disabled' – with the connotation that you can only 'beg' cap in hand if you are disabled), as well as offensive ('jungle boy' for 'black').

The terms 'gender', 'ethnicity', 'disability', 'sexuality' and 'age' are the most accurate terms when referring to categories which are associated with discrimi-nation as discrimination results from 'social' attitudes to certain groups of people. These are the groups of people who face discrimination. These are also the terms which have been chosen by discriminated groups themselves. Using these terms is a recognition of a group's own feelings of identity. Words we use are often social constructs. Society's view of women is not purely in biological terms but refers to what our society considers a woman or a man. 'Women' and 'men' conjures up more than biological differences. Women are seen as weak, caring and home lovers, men are seen as strong with drive and ambition. There is a difference between the biological meaning of male and female and the social connotations of men and women. That women bear children is a biological fact; that they earn on average three-quarters of the average male wage is not. The latter is a result of the way society functions and is not related to sexual difference but to social difference. 'Gender' is therefore a better term to denote men and women than 'sex' which has purely biological meaning. The term 'ethnicity' is more accurate than terms such as race which might imply a biological definition. In reality it is very doubtful that a biological definition could ever be given of race. This is different in this respect from the term 'sex'. The term race was given a pseudo-scientific meaning by white people to justify the oppression of black and minority ethnic people. Its usage has changed and it is now commonly used to mean people of different ethnic origin. 'Ethnicity' has a different connotation from 'race' since it refers to groups sharing a common heritage, culture or religion. White people have an ethnicity too (the Irish, the Scots and the English are all different ethnic groups). 'Gender', 'ethnicity' and 'race' are all socially constructed. 'Disability' has the same connotation: it refers to the way society views impairment and therefore has a social meaning and not simply a medical view of someone's ability. 'Homosexuality' is a medical term referring to sexual relationships; 'sexuality' is broader and carries with it a social meaning. 'Age' is also a social construct in as much as it does not denote merely chronological age but also society's views and attitudes towards different age groups. People from within these groups are 'women', 'minority ethnic people' (to denote those who belong to an ethnic group which is in a minority), 'disabled people', 'older people' and 'lesbians and gay men'.

In terms of ethnicity 'black people' is a term often used instead of 'minority ethnic people' to denote people who experience racism because of their skin colour. In the UK 'black people' can refer to those of African, Caribbean and Asian origins. 'Black' is often called a political term to refer to its social construct (the history of oppression of black people including slavery).

Racism, the belief that black people are inferior to white people, is then different from xenophobia or discriminatory practices such as anti-semitism which refer either to all those of a different ethnicity from one's own or to one specific ethnic group (Jewish).

Is this political correctness?

It is often said that being pedantic about which terms to use is either a waste of time (as it is only a cosmetic change and does not lessen discrimination) or just 'political correctness'. I have never been sure of what 'political correctness' is supposed to mean but in my view it is a derogatory term used to belittle efforts to combat discrimination by the use of accurate language. As said above, the use of appropriate terms is important for proper communication, and courtesy (addressing people in the way they wish to be addressed) is more important than burying one's head in the sand and claiming that language does not matter. But as we have seen language itself can be discriminatory. Language is very powerful; it can be used to include your audience or make people feel excluded or insulted. Equal opportunities is about changing people's attitudes, and this includes use of language, and challenging definitions of what is normally acceptable when in fact words are being used to perpetuate or justify discrimination. Words can be used to exercise power and control. If a group is excluded from society using words that ignore the existence of a group, or are denigrating to that group, this exclusion is reinforced. Constant use of the word 'man' to mean 'men and women' does exclude women. 'Chairman' is an interesting example: in the past the term 'chair' (gender neutral) was often used. In the nineteenth century when women's rights became curtailed (no right to property and so on), the term 'chairman' was introduced to reinforce control over women. However, 'chair' continued to be used in universities (the 'chair' of a faculty). It is interesting that when people object to women's use of the term 'chair' ('I am not a piece of furniture') they never feel the need to object to its use by male professors. Nor does anyone seem to object to the use of 'the bench' at a magistrates' court (it would be fun to hear the same people who object to 'chair' refuse to address 'the bench' on the grounds that a bench is a piece of furniture – and the same point can be made about 'the whip' in Parliament). The point here is that it is only the use of such terms to challenge male power which is seen as unacceptable. The fact that 'man' is not a generic term is clearly illustrated by the nonsense of the following example: 'Man suffers from backache, he ruptures easily and has difficulty in giving birth.' The term 'handicap' is discriminatory partly for the reason given above – it connotes the need for charity (to beg and put your 'cap in hand') – and partly because it means that disability can only be seen in terms of functional limitation which ignores its social dimension (the way society disables people). 'Handicapped' is therefore offensive. One way of combating discrimination is to attempt to use words which do not perpetuate discrimination.

However, it does not matter if someone does not know what the current 'right' terminology is. It does not matter if you get things wrong on occasion, so long as there is an effort not to say things which discriminate. I believe the rule is to ensure that what you are saying will not be offensive to your audience. If you are not sure what people want to be called, ask them. Many Asian people do not like being called 'black'. In such cases I would refer to them as Asian if that is what they prefer. Tariq Modood (1997) analyses research showing that whereas most African Caribbeans identify with skin colour and the term 'black', only a fifth of Asians do. Others identify themselves by nationality or religion (e.g. 'Pakistani', 'Hindu'). If I am with a group of older people who wish to be called 'pensioners', I call them 'pensioners'. I don't think it is helpful to 'correct' others when they use words about themselves different from those described above. If there is good evidence that they are being offensive (that their audience finds their use of words offensive), then it is worth pointing this out to them afterwards. But making someone feel embarrassed in front of others makes every one embarrassed and blocks communication. This is the attitude that is sometimes referred to as 'p.c.', and indeed such an attitude is not helpful. Shaming people is not a good way to get them to learn. All words change their meaning over time as language is a living tool. Groups of people often redefine themselves and give themselves a new 'name'. I am not sure why others find this so difficult. It doesn't really matter so long as one is sensitive and accepts that we all make mistakes and that this is a learning experience for all of us. The important thing is to be flexible and prepared to change.

Stereotyping people is a form of discrimination

As said many times in this chapter, difference matters. Seeing everyone the same is discriminatory. But it is not just a question of acknowledging that women, black and minority ethnic people, disabled people, older people and lesbians and gay men are different groups. We need to recognize that not all people within these groups are of a kind. Women are not a homogeneous group: some are young, some are black or from a minority ethnic group, some are disabled and so on. Disabled people are not all in wheelchairs: some are blind, deaf or have learning disabilities. And yet, when difference is recognized the tendency is to stereotype. Women in illustrations will often be portrayed as 'pretty young blondes', disabled people invariably as wheelchair users. Asian people will be in a sari or with a turban. Stereotypes can also be in associated characteristics of a certain group: 'Jamaicans are lazy' or 'Muslims are fanatical'. In terms of ethnicity, stereotypes apply to certain groups. I recently heard a North African interviewed on the radio in Paris. The same stereotypes exist there. He said that whenever French people see him they see a 'North African, and beneath that an Arab, beneath the Arab they see a Muslim, and beneath that a fundamentalist, and beneath the fundamentalist a terrorist, so when they see me they see a terrorist'. The media often portray negative stereotypes of groups of people – gay men are seen as ineffective, 'limp wristed' men or as child molesters. Stereotypes such as these are discriminatory and fuel prejudice. Language and stereotypical views can perpetuate myths which in turn give an inaccurate view of reality. 'Take the example of rape . . . It is surrounded by numerous myths: that women secretly want to be raped, that a struggling woman cannot be raped, that rapists cannot help themselves'

(McDowell and Pringle 1992: 12). These myths affect the way people treat rape. They affect behaviour. Stereotypical beliefs are used to justify inequality. The experience of inequality leads people to accept the stereotypical beliefs as true, these in turn affect behaviour and discrimination is continued. Discrimination occurs 'because those who discriminate share erroneous or stereotypical beliefs about the people they wish to exclude or victimise. In short the people who are discriminated against are *categorised* and are no longer treated as individuals with their own talents or personalities' (Blakemore and Drake 1996: 9).

Equal opportunities and diversity

Throughout this book, I have argued that equal opportunities is about combatting discrimination and that discrimination is about the way certain groups of people are treated. There is a view that difference is the cause of discrimination but that this is not *group* difference but *individual* difference. The 'managing diversity' view sees policy development in terms of individuals and not groups. Kandola, Fullerton and Ahmed say: 'Diversity includes virtually all ways in which people differ, not just the obvious ones of gender, "race" and ethnicity, disability, etc.' (1995: 31). The argument is that groups can actually be ignored in implementing equal opportunities and all emphasis should be on the individual: 'If organisations can ensure that they are able to treat individuals fairly, and they are able to respond flexibly to individual needs, they do not need to worry about groups. Equal opportunities should look after itself' (Ross and Schneider 1992: 51). Such a view of 'diversity' fails to explain discrimination. How can you explain domestic violence without reference to 'gender', or racial harassment without reference to 'race'? If you are attacked because of the colour of your skin, it isn't just because of this 'individual' characteristic, it is because of your membership of the group 'black and minority ethnic people' and all its connotations (what black and minority ethnic people are seen to be about). By using the above view of 'diversity' you lose explanatory power. Certain experiences people have cannot be explained, they therefore will not be dealt with and discrimination will not be tackled. A lot of the work done in equal opportunities presupposes the existence of groups and group characteristics. One could not have preferential treatment (positive action as allowed by the law – see Chapter 3) such as swimming sessions for women only. The view of 'diversity' as being 'individuals only' is a view not dissimilar to the belief that there is no such thing as society but only individuals (as expressed by Margaret Thatcher). Other views about 'diversity' seem to encompass all that has been said above about discrimination and represent just another term for 'equal opportunities'.

Sections below will look at different groups and how discrimination affects them.

Women

Discrimination on the grounds of gender is 'sexism'. Sexism includes be-haviour that reinforces the role of women as secondary to men. This includes behaviour that stereotypes women as inferior, or language which excludes women. Women have traditionally not been associated with 'citizenship' but with 'family life'. They are not seen as part of the public arena:

> The prevailing ideology was that men would govern the society and women the homes within it. The result was a model of social life that separated the 'private' domestic sphere from the 'public' sphere, reflected in and influenced by nineteenth-century social theory and the developing disciplines of the social sciences. Contemporary nineteenth-century no-tions of the obligations and duties of fatherhood and motherhood further reinforce the domestic/public separation and women's dependence on men because of their status as non-citizens. These assumptions continue to be reflected in contemporary legislation and social welfare policies.
>
> (McDowell and Pringle 1992: 15)

Women still are largely defined in relation to men; they are usually (in the media) referred to as someone's wife, mother or daughter. Until recently citizens' rights only applied to the public sphere. Women have increasingly fought to have this extended to the private sphere and include issues such as domestic violence which used not to be seen as a public concern. Indeed, in the 1970s when called to an incident the police would say 'Its just a domestic' and not interfere. Nowadays many police stations have domestic violence (DV) units and consider domestic violence a crime (although in law domestic violence in itself is not a crime).

Throughout the world women are amongst the poorest members of society. It is still the case that 'women constitute one half of the world's population, perform nearly two-thirds of its work hours, receive one-tenth of the world's income, and own less than one-hundredth of the world's property' (United Nations 1995). Worldwide, poverty is increasingly female. This of course includes the UK where women still earn on average (in spite of the Equal Pay Act) three-quarters of the average male wage. This figure has not substantially changed since the last century. Women are housed in the worst housing available, most council tenants are women and women have greater difficulty getting housing when they are street homeless: 'one authority has 500 bed-spaces for homeless men and only 33 for homeless women' (LGMB 1991: 25). Sports centres attract mainly men and the media rarely report on women's events. Discrimination against women is rife in the health services where women are likely to be 'labelled' by GPs as 'problems' and stereotypical views still affect the service women receive. For example, the current leaflet pro-duced by the Stroke Association, *Sex after Stroke Illness* (leaflet S16), has a section called 'Try to make it easy' which says, 'The other way to avoid problems is to try to make the actual act as easy as possible. This means letting the well partner take the most active part. This is easier if the patient is the woman, because the man does most of the moving.' This is an assumption based on the stereotypical view that women are passive. In the criminal justice system women still get a raw deal. Women are more likely to be imprisoned for fewer convictions than men: '53 per cent of women have two or fewer convictions when they first go to prison as against 22 per cent of men', and yet their offences are also usually less serious (Kennedy 1993: 22). Women who commit crimes are labelled 'mad' as opposed to 'bad', and emotionally unstable. Women also do not get proper damages for personal injury as their work is frequently unpaid ('housework' and 'childcare'). Women who sue rapists for compensation usually get less than people who sue for damages in road accidents. Helena Kennedy gives the example of a man who had a road accident, following which he was responsible for a series of sexual assaults. 'After his trial in 1983, Mr Meah was imprisoned for life, but the following year he received £45,750 compensation for his motor accident. His first victim received £1,000 from the Criminal Injuries Compensation Board, his second £3,600' (1993: 28). A man's car is still frequently seen as more valuable than his 'woman'. Local Community Safety Partnerships are often set up consisting entirely of men. They then frequently draw up a list of 'priorities' (which are not that different from priorities for crime at a national level). The highest priorities tend to be burglary and car theft. In fact there are on average three times as many domestic violence incidents than cars stolen, but for insurance reasons car theft is reported to the police at nearly 100 per cent and domestic violence at 20 per cent (no one gets insurance for domestic violence). As domestic violence is further down the list of priorities than car theft and yet three times as common, one could say that women's safety is one-third as valuable as a car. Violence against women is one of the clearest areas in which discrimination against women is still rarely tackled adequately.

Women experience violence primarily from their partners or ex-partners or from men they know, rarely from strangers. Domestic violence which occurs in the 'private' domain has long been seen as legitimate: 'Far from protecting women from it, the law has historically sanctioned the abuse of women within marriage as an aspect of the husband's ownership of his wife and his right to chastise her "with a stick no thicker than his thumb"' (Kennedy 1993: 93). And yet if someone broke your ribs what difference does it make if this happened at home or in the street? It was *legal* to rape a women within marriage till 1992. Until recently the police did not take action and even now are cautious: 'The police, who would have no problem entering premises believed to contain explosive substances, become very sensitive to the rights of man when the information relates to domestic violence' (Kennedy 1993: 83). Although the police are slowly getting their act together, many agencies are not and largely underestimate the violence women face (the courts and the health service for example). Women still face discrimination in such cases. A judge sentencing a man who twice raped his ex-wife said: '. . . a rare sort of rape. It is not like someone being jumped on in the street. This is within the family and does not impinge on the public' (Kennedy 1993: 121).

Women, among other groups of people, are afraid to go out at night for fear of attack. Improved services such as lighting, open vistas and police presence do make a difference. In 1993 when a serial rapist was loose in a small New

Zealand town, women were asked to stay indoors after dark. Next day, after dark, the women of the town marched to the Town Hall demanding that the curfew be on men not women, as the offender was a man. The point is clear: it is women who were being discriminated against in such cases.

To improve services for women, their needs must be taken into account, including childcare (for example, the provision of crèches and areas where children can play whilst their mothers access the service), parking spaces for pushchairs, accessibility by public transport, freedom from harassment and good lighting.

Black and minority ethnic people

'Racism' is the belief that people from some races are innately inferior to others. Discrimination on the grounds of ethnicity alone is 'prejudice' ('anti-Irish' etc.). Because of racism and prejudice, black and minority ethnic people are often in lower paid jobs or poor housing, get poor health provision, face harsher treatment by the police and the courts and are subject to violence (racial harassment). Different minority ethnic groups (e.g. Bangladeshi, Pakistani, Indian) face different forms of discrimination. These differences have been highlighted in a recent study: 'the main conclusion of the study is that minority ethnic groups should no longer be seen to be all in the same position. Some minorities, and some groups within a minority are doing well . . . In previous decades the focus was on a black–white divide, which emphasised the various minorities' common experience of racial exclusion. While that was, and remains, an important theme, it is now clear that the characteristics and experiences of the different minority groups require a more complex analysis' (Modood *et al.* 1997: 2).

Unemployment is higher among the black and minority ethnic population: in 1991 when the unemployment figures were 9 per cent, they were 18 per cent for African Caribbean people, 27 per cent for Africans, 29 per cent for Pakistanis and 32 per cent for Bangladeshis. Most of these groups are involved in manual work (see Modood 1994: 2). A study in Nottingham showed that 'while the unemployment rate was 19 per cent across the whole of the city, among Afro-Caribbean men aged 16–24 the figure is 41 per cent. In the late 1980s, women of Indian origin were two-thirds more likely to possess a degree qualification than the average for their sex – but were also two-thirds more likely to be unemployed' (IPPR 1993: 16). This indicates that there is clear discrimination in the job market.

Black and minority ethnic people are more likely to be in poor housing: 'White families are four to five times more likely than Black and minority ethnic applicants to have inner city houses allocated to them than flats' (LGMB 1991: 25). For many years local authorities have practised a 'sons and daughters' policy which means that if your parents live on an estate, you have priority for housing on that estate over those from outside the estate. This policy – still continued today in many places – in effect results in the 'nicer' estates remaining 'white' whilst the 'nastier' ones become 'black'. Asian families experience more overcrowding than families from other ethnic groups: for example in the London Borough of Croydon 15 per cent are living in overcrowded conditions compared with 6 per cent in the non-Asian population (London Research Centre 1997). These are clear examples of discrimination in the way council services are delivered.

Black and minority ethnic groups experience poorer health. There are, however, variations between different minority ethnic communities, with Pakistanis and Bangladeshis having poorer health than other minority ethnic groups. They had 'a 50 per cent greater risk of fair or poor health than whites. Caribbeans had a risk of fair or poor health 30 per cent greater than whites. But Indians and African Asians, like the Chinese, have levels of health very similar to the general population' (Modood *et al.* 1997: 3). This is because of racism. An experiment in Sandwell showed that addressing racism and informing health promotion workers of the needs of the black and minority ethnic community, as well as involving the community itself, improved their health. Jenny Douglas demonstrated that when seminars were organized on food and sport which were culturally appropriate (e.g. women-only swimming or Bhangra aerobics sessions), health could improve; she found that 'white health professionals lacked awareness of Asian and African Caribbean foods and therefore perpetuated racist stereotypes about unhealthy Asian and Caribbean food customs and practices' (1996: 191). Hospitals rarely provide food that is adequate for many minority ethnic groups, which means that their families have to bring in appropriate food. This is discriminatory. Other medical practices which discriminate are more serious and linked to diagnosis. For example, there is an assumption that black Caribbean men are more likely to be schizophrenic than other ethnic groups. They are indeed more often diagnosed in the UK as schizophrenic, but there are no similar high numbers in the Caribbean itself. This suggests that the diagnoses are based on racist assumptions. The impact for service provision of misdiagnosis is great. In response to discriminatory practices in housing and in health care, there has been an increase in black and minority ethnic housing associations and health provision based on non-European traditions of medicine and therapy. The latter has developed particularly in the voluntary sector. For example, in the London Borough of Hounslow a very successful organization, EACH (Ethnic Alcohol and Counselling Hounslow), provides culturally sensitive counselling in Asian languages for those with alcohol or drug problems and other related health issues.

In education, black Caribbean boys are more likely to be excluded from school, under-selected and under-represented in higher education (Modood 1994: 3), and black Caribbean children are more often taken into care. Black Caribbean men are disproportionately over-represented in the prison population and the police are more likely to stop and question black men than any other group in the population (Modood 1994: 3). Research in the London Borough of Croydon looked at the perceptions of 42 African and Caribbean 11- to 16-year-olds. The recurring themes were that the children felt they were treated differently by white teachers (and this was linked to the way society treated them outside school), they were labelled and not listened to. They were subject to racist name calling and bullying by other students. Examples of this included being called 'nigger', 'wog', 'chocolate biscuit', 'monkey' and 'Paki'.

The children felt that these taunts were not taken seriously by teachers. Invariably this led to fighting (particularly by the boys) and being excluded. They said of the fighting that it 'stressed them'. When asked what this meant, they said that the name calling 'hurt' and was deeply 'personal', implicating their families too: 'You feel as if it affects your family as well, because if they are calling you a name it means they're calling your mum and dad a name, if it's directed at you, it's directed at them' (Smith 1997). In 1987 the Commission for Racial Equality found that a higher education institution blatantly discriminated in selection of students for interview by giving lower marks to students who appeared to be non-white from the university application forms. A computer program had been created by the Medical School to mimic the selection method used by humans. If a 'foreign' sounding name (usually Asian or African) was entered, the student was given a different score by the computer. This meant that the student was less likely to be called for interview and so be admitted to the college to study medicine. No doubt this practice continues in some organizations today. This is an example of how racism can operate without those who are responsible even being consciously aware of what is going on.

Racial harassment (racial attacks) seem to be on the increase although it may be that reporting rates are going up. There were an estimated 140,000 cases in 1992 (Modood 1994: 2) and reported incidents have doubled since 1988 and increased by 8 per cent in 1996 (*Equalities News* 1996: 2). Reporting rates are low (10 per cent according to the British Crime Survey 1994). A residents' survey in the London Borough of Hounslow showed that the real figure is as high as one person in three (1994). Women are much more likely to experience racial harassment than men. As a result of fear of attack 'One in three Asian residents – 51 per cent of Asian women – *always* avoid going out after dark, three in ten Asian women *never* venture out alone. Over one in three Asian women never use buses or trains' (Newham residents' survey, quoted by LGMB 1991: 85). The same survey showed that whilst 68 per cent of women in general were worried about being the victim of a sexual assault, this rose to 81 per cent among Asian women.

When planning services for black and minority ethnic people it is important to take into account the fact that there are huge differences between different ethnic groups. Indians have different needs from Bangladeshis and Caribbeans from Africans etc. Within Africans, Somalis will have different needs from Nigerians and so on. The important factor is to be aware that no groups are homogeneous and to be sensitive to the fact that there are groups within groups. Harassment, language, diet, non-traditional sports and respect for religious difference (for example when providing burial arrangements) are all important issues. In the case of interpreters it is important to follow best practice and only use trained interpreters (not family members), particularly in situations where information given may be confidential. Many organizations now have codes of practice for interpreters and translators (there is a London-wide code available from the Association of London Government: ALG 1997b).

Disabled people

Unlike gender and ethnicity, disability is something which any one of us could develop. Some degree of disability will exist at some time in all of us. Older people make up the largest group of disabled people. This means that by tackling discrimination on the grounds of disability we will all individually benefit at some time in our lives. Until recently society's attitude to disabled people has been to offer compensation through charity and separate service provision. A commonly held view is that disabled people do not experience discrimination; it is just that they have physical and mental 'problems' which mean that they cannot use the environment and various facilities in the same way as the rest of us. The problem, it is argued, is disabled people themselves rather than a society which discriminates. For these reasons legislation for disabled people was resisted for a long time and when it was finally introduced in 1996 it was not based on an idea of 'equal rights'. Unlike the legislation for gender and ethnicity, this legislation does not take a view which is based on people's 'right' to jobs and services (the Disability Discrimination Act is described in Chapter 3). At present disability means that your choice is restricted – if you are a wheelchair user you cannot have the seat you would like in a theatre and you cannot easily take the bus, train or tube at most stations in London.

Disabled people have fought hard to shift society's view of disability away from 'charity' and towards 'rights'. The attitude of society still is that disabled people are 'handicapped' and need our help and pity; they are rarely viewed as people in their own right who are as much entitled to jobs and services as anyone else. A paternalistic attitude still prevails according to which someone needs to act on behalf of disabled people: 'disabled people cannot be trusted to organise their own services, and if they did so, demands would increase. It is thought that professionals are needed to act as assessors and gatekeepers' (Massie 1994: 23). This has been the philosophy behind most of the care provided to disabled people. Community care has not operated in a way which enables disabled people to choose their own care arrangements and be given the finance to do so. The disability movement has been successful in campaigning against the 'charitable' view of a 'benevolent' society and has stopped the awful spectacle of 'poor disabled people' being at the centre of huge popular entertainment on television (programmes appealing to the public to 'pity' disabled people and give to charity). The movement is continually arguing for 'rights not charity', a political issue rather than a social problem. Organizations campaigning on disability should be 'of' disabled people not 'for' disabled people. There is an important distinction between organizations controlled by disabled people themselves and those that are controlled by able-bodied people.

There are two different views of what disability is. One is referred to as the 'medical model', the other as the 'social model' of disability. Conventionally the problem is seen to rest with disabled people themselves who have 'something wrong with them' (a medical condition) rather than with a society which does not recognize disabled people's rights to enjoy the same things able-bodied people do (a disabling society): 'Whether or not it is intended, the unjust society is also the disabling society. The "problem" for disabled people is often judged as the physical or mental disability itself rather than the ways in which barriers are erected (or simply unchallenged), making the disability truly disabling' (Massie 1994: 3). Disability has more to do with society than medicine; the extent to which someone is disabled depends on the environment in which they live: 'The effects of disability would be reduced significantly if we decided to plan our buildings and institutions in a manner which takes account of the needs of every citizen, including those with disabilities' (Massie 1994: 6). This is not to suggest that disability would disappear if conditions in society allowed. Rather that discrimination would disappear. You would still, for example, have the pain of arthritis but you would be able to use public transport. If the problems disabled people face are seen as the domain of doctors and not policy makers, little is likely to change to improve the lives of disabled people who will be seen as 'deviants', remaining outside civil society, and who will not be involved in decisions which would influence the world we all live in: 'The medical classification of disabled individuals can tell us nothing at all about the social and physical barriers which serve to disable them . . . social attitudes and institutions, by their very nature, serve to disable people' (Blakemore and Drake 1996: 144). Policy makers need to make policies that include disabled people in such a way that buildings, education, transport are accessible to all people rather than promoting a welfare-based intervention where policies result in a segregated society in which disabled people have decisions made for them about their lives. Benefits awarded to disabled people should be on the basis of rights of citizenship and not charity: 'People are disabled not by their impairments, but by the contours and attitudes of society at large . . . In redefining the nature of disability, disabled people are asserting that they are a disadvantaged and oppressed minority group whose unequal economic and social position stems from discrimination and lack of access to power' (Leach 1989: 66).

Personal mobility can be difficult for people with disabilities. For example, 53 per cent of wheelchair users have difficulty getting around and over three-quarters feel excluded from enjoying things other people take for granted. Thirty-four per cent of wheelchair users have been turned away from a cinema and 23 per cent have been refused service in a restaurant or café (figures from Scope 1996). Improved signing helps people with hearing impairment. On the roads, pedestrians are being helped similarly by dropped kerbs, improved visual contrast and different surface materials. These are important for mobility within buildings too where Braille in lifts and voice announcements for floors helps. Induction loops and minicoms are becoming more commonly used in meeting areas and offices. All new buildings (following an extension to the Buildings Regulations in 1987) must take into account the needs of disabled people. Without this, disabled people can be denied even the opportunity to exercise their right to vote. In the 1997 general election only 6 per cent of polling stations were fully accessible according to a survey by Scope (Brindle 1997).

Disabled people experience discrimination in housing where segregated services are still frequently the norm. Some disabled people do not have the option of a home of their own and are forced to live in institutions. Some local authorities and housing associations now adapt ground floor flats for disabled people including fitting electric sockets waist high. New housing will often include flats for disabled people. Local authorities have a duty to assist people to adapt their homes under the Chronically Sick and Disabled Persons Act (1970). Since 1990, local authorities have been able to give Disabled Facilities Grants to adapt homes. This however is means tested and not all accommodation is adaptable. There is still a lack of information on both these Acts which in itself restricts access to them. When looking for accommodation it is not unusual for local authorities and estate agents not to know which of their flats and houses are accessible to those with mobility impairment (see Massie 1994: 16).

Disabled students face discrimination in education. Many children are still directed to special schools when they could be in mainstream education. Other children whose needs should be assessed do not get the service because of budget constraints (Massie 1994: 11). Further Education and Higher Education are beginning to adapt their courses for disabled students. In health, where one would assume services were geared towards the needs of disabled people, it is still the case that many hospitals are not accessible. Police stations and dentists' surgeries are also not always accessible to wheelchair users.

In transport, there is still much discrimination against disabled people. Walking is not an option for those with severe mobility difficulties who can only use a mechanical means of transport. This can be expensive since most public transport is not accessible. The London black taxi cabs can now accommodate wheelchair users, and here the private sector is ahead of the public sector. Over the last few years, buses which can be entered at pavement level have been introduced, thus making them accessible for wheelchair users, older people and parents with pushchairs. This is a good example of how proper design can benefit all. British Rail is improving its facilities. New trains now have toilets for disabled people and colour contrast is added for those who are visually impaired. In 1997 Air UK asked a disabled passenger whether he 'smelled'. He had notified the airline that he had multiple sclerosis and was a wheelchair user. The form sent by the airline asked, 'Is patient in any way offensive to other passengers (smell, appearance, conduct)?' After complaining the disabled passenger did receive an apology (see Daniels 1997).

Considering the needs of disabled people includes providing induction loops, minicoms, information in large print, surroundings with colour contrast, clear paths and pavements and good facilities at premises such as sports centres. Some guides exist to help disabled people visiting certain areas. Quiller Press produces an *Access in London* (1996) guide which gives information about travel, accommodation, leisure (including pubs) and tourist attractions in London. The Edinburgh Festival guide gives notes on access for each venue including access from the street, toilet provision, seating, bookings etc. Communication companies like British Telecom now offer a range of facilities for disabled customers with hearing, sight and speech disabilities and for those with mobility and dexterity impairment. Marks and Spencer has produced a guide for staff on dealing with disabled customers. The guide aims to raise awareness about disability among staff: 'Being disabled is not the same as being ill. Most disabled people are perfectly well. People with disabilities don't always have problems getting around – less than 5 per cent use wheel-chairs. You can't always tell if a person is disabled just by looking at them. Some people may have disabilities you can't see, such as deafness or mental health difficulties' (Employers' Forum on Disability 1996: 2). The guide also offers advice: 'Don't describe a disabled person in terms of a condition like "Mary is a spastic". Don't use words that make disabled people seem frail or dependent, like "victim of", "crippled by" or "suffering from". Keep it simple. Just say what the person has: "Mary had epilepsy", "John has MS"' (Employers' Forum on Disability 1996: 4).

Older people

Like disability, old age is something we might all experience. Barring prema-ture death we will all grow old. Tackling discrimination on the grounds of age will benefit everyone. Age discrimination is about treating people less favour-ably on the grounds of their assumed chronological age. This can start in middle age where for example you cannot get a mandatory grant for higher education if you are over 50 years old. Typically older people are patronized, 'little old ladies', and seen as helpless and dependent on society's (or their family's) goodwill. Older people do have genuine needs concerning services such as housing, health and leisure, but these can only be tackled if 'age' itself is not seen as a problem. We need to acknowledge that the problem is the way society sees older people. At present the common view is that older people live in nursing homes when in fact 95 per cent of those over 65 live in their own homes. We are obsessed with questions of senility and Alzheimer's disease and yet less than 5 per cent of people over 65 experience either of these. Betty Friedan quotes these and other figures in *The Fountain of Age* and says: 'Why the persistent image of age as "sick" and "helpless", as a burden on our hospitals and health care systems, when, in fact, people over sixty-five are less likely than those who are younger to suffer from the acute illnesses that require hospitalization? Why the persistent image of those over sixty-five as sexless when research shows people capable of sex until ninety?' (1994: 32). Friedan analyses the negative images society has of older people. If not nega-tive, older people simply do not figure: there are very few positive images of older people in the media. More often they are portrayed as objects of fun and ridicule ('grumpy old men', 'bigoted old women'). These attitudes are dis-criminatory because they mean that older people will be denied the services they need because of prejudice.

As they are not seen as being entirely in charge of their faculties, older people are often infantilized and treated as children ('second childhood'). This can be seen by the way older people are often talked to in residential homes: 'Be a good girl and eat up.' In this way older people are denied choices other people would be given. Betty Friedan describes an experiment in the US in which older people in a nursing home were divided into two groups. Those in one group were allowed to decide how their rooms were decorated and arranged, given plants to choose and look after, asked when they wanted to see their friends, when they wanted to go to the cinema and what they wanted to see. Those in the other group had their rooms decorated and arranged for them, plants given to them and watered by the nurses and they were told when visiting hours would be, when films would be shown and what films they would be. After three weeks, all of those in the first group showed signs of improvement, only 21 per cent of those in the second group did. A year and a half later, 15 per cent of those in the first group had died and 30 per cent of those in the second group. In addition 'the survivors who exercised their own choices were now significantly superior to the others on measures of physical and psychological health' (1994: 53). This example illustrates how the pervasive image of older people as 'people in decline' is discriminatory and means that older people get a raw deal.

Older people are amongst the poorest in society and have less access to services than most. Many are completely dependent on state benefits: 'Those at most risk of significant poverty include those over the age of 80, women, those living alone and disabled elders' (O'Neill 1996: 35). Poverty limits choice and forces older people into dependence. Age Concern found that VAT on fuel meant that 37 per cent of pensioners at the lowest income level had to reduce spending on food and clothing to pay fuel bills (quoted by O'Neill 1996: 35).

Health care services for older people are frequently discriminatory. Many illnesses which could be treated are blamed on 'old age' and older people themselves internalize this view and put up with their ailments. A study which concentrated on improving access to health services for older people (access to hospital and social workers) by encouraging self-referral found that 50 per cent of those over 75 had sensory, cognitive and/or physical impairments which had not been assessed. Their problems were not dealt with as they were seen as 'normal' for their age group (see O'Neill 1996: 52ff). There is a widespread assumption that there is no need to treat certain conditions in older people (sexual dysfunction) or prioritize them for certain operations (kidney transplant), as if their lives were somehow less worthy of care than those of the rest of the population. The argument is that they are due to die shortly anyway. This ignores the fact that many older people have 10 to 20 years of life left and in addition the 'quality' of one's life is not in any way related to 'quantity': 'Much ageism stems from ignorance about the value of . . . interventions in later life' (O'Neill 1996: 39). This occurs for example with heart conditions: 'In the first few hours after a heart attack, many older people have previously been excluded from therapy which dissolves a clot in the artery . . . A major international study showed that in fact older people gain more benefit from this therapy than younger people' (O'Neill 1996: 39). It also occurs with breast screening. Routine breast screening is a national policy in Britain for women between the ages of 50 and 65. Women over 65 are not invited but can refer themselves. Those who do face considerable barriers and only 2 per cent are screened. Ageism in the NHS is also demonstrated by the fact that when a 5 per cent increase pushes the 50- to 65-year-olds' figure for screening up to 75 per cent this is considered a success, yet if over 65-year-olds' self-referrals increase to 5 per cent it is seen as an extra burden (see Sutton 1997: 1032). We need to reassess our view of the value of older people's lives just as we had to reassess our views on the value of children's lives in the early part of the twentieth century. As O'Neill says: 'One in two Victorian children died in the first eight

years of life: this fact was accepted by society as normal. Pioneering paedia-
tricians faced a battle reminiscent to that of early geriatricians to prioritise the
fight against childhood disease. They did not concentrate only on the medical
problems of childhood but they also acted as powerful advocates for change in
social attitudes' (1996: 34). A similar change needs now to occur in respect of
'age'.

For these reasons, leisure services are rarely geared towards older people. The
Local Government Management Board gives an example of a discriminatory
leisure centre. This would be one which only employed young, healthy
looking staff, had security on the door as if expecting trouble, had no seating
in the centre, used as much 'technology' as possible, had no concessionary
prices, and did not run special classes in the daytime except on the day
pensioners collect their pensions! The image of the centre was one that
emphasized 'youth', stressed 'activity' and had publicity in small print. The
centre was far from public transport, had poor lighting, lots of steps, poor
visibility inside and loud background music. The café was expensive, promoted fast food, had disco-pub lighting and music and theme nights such as
'vicars 'n' tarts' (LGMB 1991: 139). Similar points can be made about education, retail and other services which do not make themselves appealing to
older people.

Taking into account the needs of older people means looking at the way
things are packaged and advertised, the way customers are welcomed, the
surroundings (safety, visibility, noise) among other things. Some service
providers understand this well. Seeboard (electricity and gas company) has a
leaflet stating that it is 'committed to providing excellent service to all its
customers' (1995) and goes on to pick out for special mention disabled people
and older people. Seeboard offers an information pack on its services for older
people including a 'temperature card' and information on bogus callers.

Lesbians and gay men

Discrimination against lesbians and gay men stems from the view that they are
in some way not 'normal'. Here 'normal' seems to have two different mean-
ings: a deviation from the norm (the average) and 'natural'. Stereotypical
views about lesbians include the belief that they cannot be mothers (it isn't
natural). In reality many lesbians become pregnant and do have children. One
reason for the defence that 'it isn't natural' is that it avoids engaging in the
topic. Once said, that is the end of the argument. It suggests that this is a
scientific fact and no more. The same used to be true when people argued for
biological differences and inequalities among the races or between men and
women ('they have smaller brains' and are therefore inferior was a commonly
held view in the last century). Stereotypical views of lesbians and gay men also
include the idea that lesbians are 'man haters' and gay men 'paedophiles'.
Neither of these views bears any relation to reality but such stereotypes do
impinge on service delivery. The views that lesbians and gay men will
'brainwash the children', are 'ridiculous people', will 'break up family life',
are 'responsible for child abuse', even 'will cause nuclear war' are all things that

have been claimed by the press in the last ten years (see London Strategic Policy Unit 1987: 6–7). The depth of prejudice and fear about lesbians and gay men can be measured by the volume of hate directed towards them. Articles in the media refer to lesbians as 'strident, aggressive, hairy-nippled feminists' (*The Star*, 24 February 1987). They are frequently called 'domineering', 'radical', 'sexually repressed', 'social misfits', 'butch' (London Strategic Policy Unit 1987: 8–9). In reality lesbians and gay men come in all shapes and sizes, all ethnic groups, all ages, classes and from all political beliefs. If gay men and lesbians show affection towards each other (in Britain), this is seen as offensive, in some cases even illegal. Long-term relationships have no legal status. Because gay men are seen as a threat to society, they are more likely to be subjected to attack ('queer bashing'). This was until recently seen as fair game and the police are only just beginning to take homophobic attacks seriously.

Housing tenancies are often not jointly issued to gay and lesbian couples which means that partners do not have the same rights to the tenancy as heterosexual couples do. Obtaining double mortgages can lead to difficulties if one partner dies. This is particularly a problem for gay men where insurance companies ask for information about HIV testing and status. Young people are often thrown out of their parents' home if they declare their sexuality. Homelessness is therefore a greater problem in the lesbian and gay community than in the community at large. As lesbians and gay men get older, their needs will not be recognized in residential homes. When couples live together, they are frequently subjected to violence and abuse: 'One lesbian couple had had excreta put through the letter box of their council flat, had had break ins, and were subsequently forced to sleep with a knife by their bedside . . . another lesbian was verbally harassed . . . by National Front supporters in adjacent neighbouring flats . . . another, living in a hostel for young single homeless people, was harassed by other residents who targeted both her and a gay male resident as Aids carriers, refusing to use crockery and cutlery that they had touched' (Anlin 1989: 5). Jane Egerton chronicles the numerous housing problems faced by lesbians in 'Out but not down: lesbian experience of housing' (1994: 197–209). In the article she describes one case: 'I once advised a Glaswegian lesbian in her seventies who had been driven from one squalid and impermanent home after another as a result of harassment from neighbours. Her family would have nothing to do with her and her only friend had been her lover who had recently died. She had never experienced the pleasures of a genuine "home" in her entire life' (1994: 198).

Health issues are either masked or exaggerated. Given that a lot of health surveys are based on couples living together, if 'couples' are defined as a man living with a woman, surveys will not have any analyses of the needs of lesbians and gay men: 'as a result, the major lifestyle surveys are silent on the question of how the domestic lives of women living with women, in sexual and non-sexual relationships, affect their eating and smoking habits and their patterns of exercise and alcohol consumption' (Graham 1996: 64). The fact that there is a differential in law between gay men and heterosexual men around the age of consent means that sexuality will be problematic for young gay men who will not have access to health information concerning their sexuality. The medical profession largely ignores the reality of lesbian and gay sexuality except to pathologize it (as in the Aids episode, where gay sex was equated with 'the gay plague'). A friend of mine recently went to a gynaecologist with a minor complaint. Among other questions, he asked her whether she had regular sex. She said that she did and added that she was a lesbian. The gynaecologist wrote on her notes 'Not sexually active'! He presumably believed 'sex' only had meaning in relation to heterosexual couples or only meant penetrative sex.

Double discrimination

Many people face not one but two or more discriminatory attitudes in their dealings with service providers. This is because people do not fit neatly into the categories outlined above. You can be both black and a woman and face discrimination on both these grounds. Examples of this would include women who experience racial harassment: there is often a 'sexist' element attached (this is borne out by statistics which show that women are disproportionately victims. See CRE 1996a: 20). For older people who are also lesbians or gay men, there are additional problems – as mentioned above – concerning housing and health. The sexuality of older people is frequently ignored and its clinical relevance missed. Disability among older people frequently goes unrecognized: 'the narrow focus of an over-specialised medical model of health is such as to place a low priority on the assessment (not to mention remediation) of physical impairment among older patients' (O'Neill 1996: 36). If problems are unrecognized and undetected they will simply not be responded to. The Commission for Racial Equality and Age Concern did a study called *Age and Race* (CRE 1995a). This showed that there are many myths and stereotypes about minority ethnic elders for whom support in terms of service provision is fragmented and marginalized from mainstream support for older people. People from Caribbean and Indian descent are the largest groups of elders, followed by Pakistani people. All will have different needs as older people. Assessing their needs may be difficult because of language barriers. The report, for example, identified that 'there is a need for greater preventive health services offering advice, support and information in alternative languages' (CRE 1995a: 9). Too many service providers assume that if a group of people do not use a service it is because they don't need it, but it is equally common for people not to know about it. It is a myth that the numbers of minority ethnic elders are small, that their families will support them or that they all return home. Lack of culturally sensitive services for older people can often result in low use even when people do know about them. In the London Borough of Hounslow where a survey was done of meals on wheels to determine why Asian elders were not using the service, the results showed quite clearly that the 'white European' food was not adequate culturally or religiously, and even 'Asian' food cooked by 'white' cooks was not adequate. Only when the food was properly prepared by the Asian community itself could Asian elders consider this a service meeting their needs. A survey by *Health Which* (1995: 206–9) of 22 local authorities showed that half provided kosher or halal meals, 20 per cent African Caribbean foods and 8 per cent Asian vegetarian food. These examples show clearly that in all cases of possible discrimination it is worth looking at areas where there could be other discriminatory factors at work. Just as older people – as we have seen – are not a homogeneous group, the same is true for disabled people, women, black and minority ethnic people and lesbians and gay men.

Conclusion

Understanding discrimination is difficult because of the complexity of the subject. However, if services are going to be appropriate to the needs of different groups of people, it is crucial to be aware of the different damaging stereotypical attitudes, outright prejudice and hostility towards different groups that will result in making genuine need go unrecognized. Different groups of people should be listened to and allowed to express their own identity and their own needs (see Chapter 4). Some complex problems will require the efforts of more than one service deliverer if they are to be tackled successfully. This is true, for example, of domestic violence or racial harassment where inter-agency work has proved more effective than each agency delivering its service in isolation of others. In these cases the police have worked with housing departments and the voluntary sector to take a co-ordinated approach and provide co-ordinated responses. The groups looked at in this chapter are by no means the only groups of people who may experience discrimination. Refugees, ex-offenders, different religious groups or working-class people, for example, also face discrimination. In talking of discrimination, it used to be common to 'rank' groups and claim that one form of 'oppression' was more serious or more fundamental to the structure of society than another. Thus, for example, 'class' was seen as more basic, 'race' more serious and so on. These divisions are not helpful. Most commonly today it is accepted that such a hierarchy of oppression simply confounds the various problems discriminated groups face. Sometimes an argument is put forward for concentrating on one area of discrimination on the basis that anti-discriminatory practices in the other areas will naturally follow. This is a nice idea but simply is not true. You can have good anti-racist practices and still be highly sexist. One example of this is the International Olympics Committee. The Committee was, rightly, quite happy to ban South Africa from participating in the games for many years on the grounds that it was a country which denied civil rights to its black population, but the Committee was and still is willing to let several middle eastern countries participate in the games in spite of the fact that they deny civil rights to women (the right to vote, to own property and so on). Similar examples could be given for other groups of people. Each form of discrimination is unique and does not often bear much relation to other forms of discrimination.

This chapter has looked at the way in which discrimination arises and is maintained. The rest of this book is concerned with developing mechanisms to counter discrimination in the delivery of services. Discrimination can be challenged at a national level, at organizational level, group level or on a personal level. National levels include anti-discriminatory legislation. One of the most powerful tools available to ensure that people's needs are met and not ignored when delivering services is the law. The next chapter looks at the anti-discrimination legislation covering different groups of people.

3

WHAT THE LAW REQUIRES

At present UK law, as it relates to service delivery, covers gender, race and disability. The three Acts covering these groups, the Sex Discrimination Act (SDA), Race Relations Act (RRA) and Disability Discrimination Act (DDA), will be looked at in this chapter. Laws on their own do not ensure good practice in equal opportunities; they do however provide a framework within which equal opportunities can work. They also provide routes for redress for those experiencing discrimination. This chapter looks at liability and case law in relation to service delivery. Why are some groups covered by legislation and not others? Although there is a long history of struggle for equal rights both the SDA and the RRA came into effect in the mid-1970s as a result of the black movement in the 1960s and the women's movement in the 1970s. These two movements raised public awareness on rights for women and for black people. The disability movement is more recent and society is only just recognizing the idea of rights for disabled people. The DDA was passed in 1995. Although the gay movement has existed for some considerable time, discrimination on the grounds of sexuality is largely unrecognized in society. There is a growing movement from older people to persuade society to acknowledge discrimination on grounds of age but this too is not yet widely understood or accepted. The chapter considers the sorts of things legislation should cover in the UK on age and sexuality. There are other legislative measures with implications for equalities which stress anti-discriminatory practices. These too are considered in this chapter.

Sex Discrimination Act (SDA)(1975)

In this chapter I shall use the term 'sex' to mean 'gender' since that is the wording of the Act. The Act is written in terms of discrimination against women but it applies equally to discrimination against men.

For goods, facilities and services the Act is clear. It is unlawful to discriminate in the provision to the public, or to a section of the public, of goods, facilities or services, either by refusing them or by providing them on less favourable terms than would be offered to members of the opposite sex (SDA s. 29). This applies to all goods, facilities and services apart from those which are exempt. It includes 'access to and use of any place which members of the public or sections of the public are permitted to enter'. Services include public services and services provided by voluntary or private agencies. Examples are housing, transport, travel, retail, restaurants, pubs, banking and finance, education, sporting facilities and clubs of at least 25 members and which are open to the public.

Some aspects of services are specified in the legislation. For example *premises*. It is unlawful to discriminate in the sale or letting of premises (SDA s. 30). This applies to public and private housing and includes land and business premises. It includes estate agents. Accordingly this legislation also covers mortgages, loans, improvement grants, rental and information and advice on housing.

Exemptions to the Act include the activities of political parties, religious organizations, non-profit making voluntary bodies and genuinely private clubs. Registered charities can also be exempt if they were set up to provide a service for one sex only. For premises, exemption includes lettings in a small dwelling where the proprietor also resides and there is shared accommodation with other persons living there (e.g. lodgings). There are also exemptions for accommodation provided for men or women only by voluntary bodies whose membership is restricted to one sex (e.g. Young Men's Christian Association).

There are four types of behaviour that are considered to be potentially unlawful under the Act:

Direct discrimination is defined under the SDA as treating someone less favourably on the grounds of sex or marital status. If a woman were treated less favourably than a man would be treated in the same circumstances this would amount to direct discrimination, for example if a restaurant refused to serve a woman and yet was happy to serve a man. Direct discrimination is unlawful under the Act (SDA s. 1(1)(*a*)).

Indirect discrimination is defined as applying a requirement or condition which, whether intentionally or not, adversely affects one sex considerably more than another, or married people more than unmarried people, and which has no objective justification. This would be the case, for example, if a public swimming pool provided changing rooms for men but not for women. In these cases it is irrelevant whether someone intended to discriminate or not. Indirect discrimination is unlawful under the Act (SDA s. 1(1)(*b*)).

Victimization counts as discrimination within the law. If someone complains about discrimination on the grounds of sex and is subsequently treated less favourably because of having complained, this is unlawful. If someone is treated in this way because they helped someone else to complain this also counts as victimization and is unlawful (SDA s. 4(1)).

To instruct or pressurize someone into acting in a discriminatory fashion on the grounds of sex or to aid someone to discriminate on these grounds is unlawful (SDA s. 39, s. 40 and s. 42).

Positive action is lawful under the Act for training. This means that it is possible to provide training for one sex only in cases where that sex has been under-represented in the occupations for which the training is provided (SDA s. 47). Training can also be provided for men or women only if they have had a break from full-time employment because of 'domestic responsibilities' (SDA s. 47(3)). What is unlawful is positive or reverse discrimination. This would be, for example, providing training for women only without justification and where there was no similar training on offer for men.

It is unlawful to advertise a service which is seen to be discriminatory, or to advertise anything 'which indicates, or might reasonably be understood as indicating, an intention by a person to do any act which is or might be unlawful' (SDA s. 38(1)). Examples would include half price entry for women- or men-only nights at a restaurant which is open to the public. The Act applies to most services which are regularly advertised: entertainment, recreation, refreshments, travel, educational courses, credit and mortgages.

The Equal Opportunities Commission (EOC) was set up under the SDA to work to eliminate discrimination and to promote equality of opportunity between men and women. It has the power to conduct formal investigations. If practices are considered by the Commission to be possibly discriminatory, it can conduct a formal investigation where, with the approval of the Secretary of State, the EOC will appoint one or more individuals to conduct a formal investigation. The terms of reference for the investigation are drawn up by the EOC or the Secretary of State. The EOC can also serve non-discriminatory notices. This could be as a result of a formal investigation or as the outcome of cases taken to the courts or tribunals under the Act. The non-discriminatory notice requires an organization not to act in the way it has and to comply with required changes in practice. The notice can also specify time limits within which changes must occur, require an organization to give evidence at hearings and provide information to the Commission such as, for example, evidence of policies, procedures and training. The EOC can also instigate judicial reviews where, for example, UK primary legislation is incompatible with European Community law. For some investigations the Commission has power to require an organization to produce information and give evidence at hearings. The Commission also gives advice generally on the Act and in some circumstances will help an individual take a case to court. This occurs, for example, if the case raises an issue of principle under the Act. The Commission can also help individuals settle a case out of court and offers legal advice.

Race Relations Act (RRA)(1976)

The first legislation against discrimination on the grounds of race was intro- duced in 1965 and revised in 1968. This became the Race Relations Act in 1976.

As with the SDA it is unlawful to discriminate in the provision to the public or to a section of the public of goods, facilities or services, either by refusing them or by providing them on less favourable terms than they would be offered to members of another race (RRA s. 20). Again this includes access to and use of any place which members of the public are permitted to enter. The Act applies to all goods, facilities and services with a few exceptions. In addition the Act makes it unlawful to segregate a person, or groups of people, on racial grounds as this would constitute 'less favourable treatment'. As with the SDA, the Act specifically mentions premises (RRA s. 21, s. 22, s. 23).

Four types of discrimination are specified:

Direct discrimination is used to mean treating a person less favourably than others on the grounds of race. 'Race' is defined as colour, nationality (including citizenship), ethnic and national origins. 'Racial group' means a group of persons defined by reference to colour, race, nationality or ethnic or national origins. The fact that a racial group comprises two or more distinct racial sub-groups does not prevent it from constituting a particular racial group for the purposes of the Act. Refusing to serve someone in a pub because they are black or having rules in a club which bar the Irish are examples of direct discrimination. Direct discrimination is unlawful under the Act (RRA s. 1(1)(*a*)).

Indirect discrimination is applying a condition or requirement for access to a service which, whether intentionally or not, adversely affects people from a particular racial group and which has no objective justification – for example, having a dress code in a club, open to the public, which did not allow the wearing of turbans. Indirect discrimination is unlawful under the Act (RRA s. 1(1)(*b*)).

Victimization counts as discrimination in the same way as with the SDA (RRA s. 2).

To instruct or pressurize someone into acting in a discriminatory fashion on the grounds of race or to aid someone to discriminate on these grounds is unlawful (RRA s. 30, s. 31, s. 33).

Positive action is lawful for training in the same way as under the SDA (RRA s. 37, s. 38). It is also lawful to address special educational, training or welfare needs identified for a specific racial group (RRA s. 35). Under s. 35 of the Act, training and education can be provided for a particular racial group if that group has different needs or greater needs than the needs of the rest of the population.

As with the SDA, it is unlawful to advertise a service which is seen to be discriminatory, or to advertise anything which appears to indicate an intention to discriminate (RRA s. 29).

In addition to the sections which are similar to the SDA, the RRA has a further section concerning local authorities. Under s. 71, local authorities have a specific responsibility to make appropriate arrangements with a view to securing that their various functions are carried out with due regard to the need to eliminate unlawful racial discrimination and to promote equality of opportunity, and good relations, between persons of different racial groups. Section 71 is not however backed by extra resources for local authorities or special sanctions. Its scope is therefore, in reality, limited.

The Commission for Racial Equality (CRE) was set up under the RRA to work to eliminate discrimination on the grounds of race and to promote equal opportunities between the races. It has the same powers as the Equal Opportunities Commission and can undertake formal investigations, serve non-discrimination notices and undertake judicial reviews.

The CRE has produced various codes of practice which apply to service provision. There is, for example, a code of practice for education which covers admissions, assessment, exclusions, work experience, careers advice, grants, fees, student accommodation and racial harassment (one code for England and Wales and another for Scotland). The CRE codes of practice are: *Rented Housing, Non-rented Housing, Elimination of Racial Discrimination in Education, Maternity Services* and *Primary Health Care Services*. The codes of practice are used in legal cases and do have the weight of law.

Disability Discrimination Act (DDA) (1995)

For many years anti-discriminatory legislation on disability was resisted by government because disabled people were not considered to experience discrimination. The only problems they were thought to face were those that resulted from their own disability, not from society's attitude towards them. Another argument used was that legislation could not work and that it would be better to win over employers by persuading them to employ disabled people. The disability movement finally managed to convince the government of the need for legislation outlawing such discrimination on the grounds of disability given that legislation is not meant to win people over but to regulate behaviour. After various drafts and much lobbying the Disability Discrimination Act came into being in 1995. It was effective from December 1996 for employment and is being introduced gradually over a number of years, starting in January 1997 with service delivery. The Act is not as straightforward as the SDA or the RRA. The definition of disability is derived from the 'medical model' of disability (see Chapter 2). For this reason disabled people are not happy with the Act because it does not recognize the way in which society 'disables' people and it does not place as strong an emphasis on rights as the SDA or RRA. The disability movement is campaigning to have the Act strengthened.

In the same way as occurs with the SDA and the RRA, the DDA prohibits discrimination against disabled people in employment, the provision of goods and services and the sale or rental of premises. In terms of services the Act applies to all services delivered to the public whether paid for or not (DDA s. 19(2). There are exclusions to the Act. Education, including further and higher education, is excluded. The only requirement in the Act is that schools, colleges and universities have to provide information about their access and disability policies. They do not have to improve their access or any of their facilities. Transport is also generally excluded with only some aspects included: the infrastructure (e.g. stations) is included but other parts of the system are not (e.g. trains, buses). The DDA does however require licensing of taxis to be granted on condition that they are accessible to all disabled people including wheelchair users (DDA s. 32). This will apply to new licences being issued. For taxis being re-licensed, they can remain non-accessible up to a specified date. Some licensing authorities can seek exemption providing clear criteria are met. Within the DDA, the Secretary of State has the power to lay down standards for transport vehicles which could be added in coming years.

Disability is defined as 'a physical or mental impairment which has a substantial and long-term adverse effect on (a person's) ability to carry out normal day to day activities' (DDA s. 4). The details of this definition are complex. It is meant to include all those who would normally be considered disabled, whether through mental illness, long-term health condition, sensory impairment, physical impairment or learning disability.

Under the Act the following would amount to discrimination:

- to refuse services to a disabled person: refusal to sell bread or to lend a book in a public library to someone who is disabled is unlawful, or refusal to serve someone in a supermarket because they take too long to collect their goods is unlawful (DDA s. 19);
- to provide services of a worse standard to a disabled person: asking someone with facial disfigurement to sit in a corner of a restaurant so as not to put off other customers is unlawful (DDA s. 19);
- to provide services to a disabled person on less favourable terms: asking a disabled person for a bigger deposit on a holiday is unlawful (DDA s. 19);
- failing to make reasonable changes or adjustments so that disabled customers can use the service (DDA s. 21). For example, if a restaurant does not allow dogs they will have to accept guide dogs. Other examples would be the introduction of an induction loop for those with hearing impairment or hand rails for those who have mobility disabilities. If it is reasonable to do so alterations such as ramps and widening of doors will need to be made. The definition of 'reasonable' is not clear (see below). If, however, the way the service is run is fundamental to the business changes do not have to be made (and discrimination is allowable). This would occur, for example, where dim light is essential to the service and yet those with sight impairment can't properly see (e.g. a nightclub).

For premises landlords cannot charge higher rent or refuse to let a room to disabled customers, although landlords who let six or fewer rooms are exempt. Those who let or sell property cannot refuse to do so to a disabled customer or charge them more, but they do not have to make it accessible for disabled people.

Discrimination is defined in a different way from the SDA and RRA. In the DDA it is defined either as less favourable treatment or a failure to consider 'reasonable adjustments' (DDA s. 1). The section on premises only uses the less favourable treatment definition of discrimination. Less favourable treatment means treating a person less favourably for reasons which relate to their disability from the way in which a person would be treated for whom these reasons did not apply. Within this definition reasons for less favourable treatment are discriminatory if they cannot be justified. This is fundamentally different from the SDA and RRA where the less favourable clause is simply 'on the grounds of' sex or race. In the DDA it is 'a reason which relates to' an individual disability. So, the comparison between the person facing discrimination and the one who is not focuses on the 'reason' for the discrimination. Under the SDA you face discrimination if someone treats you less favourably just because you are a woman. Under the DDA you face discrimination if someone treats you less favourably for a reason that 'relates' to your disability. This in effect means that the distinction made in the SDA and the RRA between direct and indirect discrimination does not apply in the DDA. Both direct and indirect discrimination come under the same heading of a reason that 'relates' to the disability. Unlike the SDA and RRA, positive discrimination is lawful under the DDA. This is because the Act applies to disabled people only and not able-bodied people. This is advantageous for disabled people. Indeed if you are disabled, you can take a complaint against a service provider if you feel that it treated an able-bodied person more favourably. But if you are able-bodied, you cannot take a case if you feel the service provider treated a disabled person more favourably. A restaurant could, for example, legally give priority service to a disabled person even if this disadvantages an able-bodied person. You cannot do this for women or for black and minority ethnic people. The RRA applies to all races (including 'white') and the SDA to both sexes. Under the DDA it is lawful to refuse a service or provide a less favourable service to an able-bodied person if this decision is made on the basis of disability.

The other difference from the SDA and RRA is that the DDA allows discrimination to be justified (DDA s. 24). The first justification is if the less favourable treatment is necessary in order not to endanger the health or safety of any person (including the disabled person). This justification has often been used before the Act came into being to bar disabled people from premises. They represent a 'fire hazard' and would be in the way if the building needed to be evacuated in a hurry. A second justification for discrimination is if the disabled person is incapable of entering into an enforceable agreement. The problem with this is that there is no single legal test which can be used to determine a person's legal capacity. This justification will also depend on the complexity of the agreement. Someone may not understand the complexity of a mortgage agreement but understand perfectly well that buying a cup of coffee involves paying a certain amount of money. A third justification for discrimination is that a service can be refused if this is necessary because the provider would otherwise not be able to provide the service to other members of the public. This 'applies only in circumstances in which, if a service provider were to serve a particular disabled person, he would not be able to continue to provide his service at all'. Being offered a less favourable service (of a lower standard) can be justified if it is necessary in order to provide the service either to the disabled person or to other members of the public. A fourth justification is where cost is incurred by the service provider in ensuring a service to a disabled customer. In such cases there can be a difference in the terms on which the service is provided to a disabled person. However, costs cannot be those which are required for 'reasonable adjustments' (see below). One of the weaknesses of this part of the Act is that service providers do not need to prove that this justification is valid, they only need to believe that it is and that it was reasonable to have such an opinion (DDA s. 20(3)).

A strength of the Act is that there is a duty on service providers to make 'reasonable adjustments' so that disabled people can use the service (DDA s. 21). Many of the barriers which have prevented disabled people having access to services can start being dismantled through this requirement of the Act. This includes changes to practices, policies or procedures; changes to physical features (removal, alterations, alternatives made available); and provision of an auxiliary aid or service (e.g. provision of information in Braille or on audio-tape for those with visual impairment or in sign language for people with hearing impairment). These requirements are to be phased in over a number of years. What counts as 'reasonable' is not clear. The government will introduce regulations giving a ceiling to what a service provider is expected to spend on adjustments (DDA s. 21(8)).

The government has set up a National Disability Council (NDC). Its role is solely to advise the Secretary of State but not to take action or provide help to disabled individuals or organizations.The NDC does not have the powers to enforce the law in the way the CRE and EOC have. A Disability Rights Commission is due to be set up before the year 2000. This will have the same powers as the CRE and EOC.

Codes of practice to give guidance on the Act have been issued. These are admissible as evidence in court in the same way as the codes of practice produced by the CRE and the EOC. There is a code of practice on access to goods, facilities, services and premises. There is also a code of practice on the definition of disability.

By and large, people in the disability movement are not happy with the DDA. They are lobbying for changes which would bring about protection in the law for all disabled people facing discrimination; a Commission with enforcement powers comparable to the EOC and CRE; schools and colleges to be included in the Act; and all forms of public transport to be made accessible.

Liability and redress

Organizations are liable under the SDA, the RRA and the DDA for any breaches in the law as it applies to service delivery. This includes liability for actions by employees. The fact that some discriminatory action occurred without the employer's knowledge is no defence in law unless the employer had taken steps to prevent such discrimination from occurring. Preventive measures would include staff training, briefing, guides on good practice and regular monitoring of customers and staff (see Chapter 6 for advice on monitoring). Organizations are also liable for actions taken by agents working on their behalf (vicarious liability). This includes agents providing services as contractors or franchisees and subsidiaries of foreign companies based in the UK (SDA s. 41, s. 50, RRA s. 32, s. 40). Management measures, such as having a policy, training on the policy and advertising the policy, will go some way towards avoiding litigation. Monitoring of customers may also help in as much as it will provide evidence of non-discrimination if an organization has proof that its customers include women, black and minority ethnic people and disabled people.

Complainants under the three Acts can take their cases to the County Courts, Magistrates or High Courts in England and Wales and to the Sheriff Courts in Scotland. There is a time limit of six months for bringing a case (some exceptions can be made if the circumstances warrant it (SDA s. 76(1)(95)(96), RRA s. 68(1)(6)(7)). Damages awarded cover financial loss and injury to feelings and courts can make orders to the organization to put matters right (e.g. change procedures and so on).

The following are examples of cases which have either been subject to an investigation by the CRE or gone to court or been settled out of court. Nearly all these examples are cases taken under the RRA but equivalent cases could be taken under the SDA or DDA, with the exception that there is no equivalent body to the CRE or EOC with powers to undertake disability discrimination investigations.

Education is clearly specified under both the SDA and the RRA where it is stated that discrimination is unlawful in the recruitment of students or provision of access to benefits, facilities or services (SDA s. 22, RRA s. 17); in provision of vocational training (SDA s. 14, RRA s. 13); or in conferring vocational or professional qualifications (SDA s. 13, RRA s. 12). In 1983, the House of Lords ruled that it was unlawful indirect discrimination for a Sikh boy who wore a turban to be banned from admission to a Birmingham school. This case rested on whether 'Sikh' counted as an ethnic group. It was decided that it did and the definition of an ethnic group was given as a community with 'a long shared history and a cultural tradition of their own'. A school in Northamptonshire County Council agreed to a wide-ranging programme of measures as part of the settlement of a complaint of racial discrimination by the parent of a black boy (1996). The settlement included payment to the complainant, training in racial discrimination for staff and governors, advice to all staff and pupils on harassment and the introduction of a complaints procedure for complaints under the RRA and SDA. In 1988 the CRE found discrimination in admission procedures in a medical college (St George's, University of London). A computer programme was selecting students for interview using information provided on the UCCA forms. Those who had names which appeared 'foreign' were given lower ranking, as were women. They were therefore less likely to be called for interview than white or male students. The CRE required the college to improve its procedures and introduce ethnic monitoring. In 1997 Dame Allen's Boys' School, a public school, was forced to apologize to a pupil for the racial harassment and bullying he had suffered whilst at the school. The school had failed to take effective action over complaints of racial abuse and physical assaults by other pupils. The boy was suspended after a fight with another pupil who called him 'black bastard'. This was after various complaints had already been made to the school by the boy's parents. The school blamed the boy and put pressure on his parents to withdraw him from the school. The school had to pay compensation to the boy and legal costs, and was also required to introduce an equal opportunities policy.

Airlines have had cases found against them in recent years. In 1996 Mr Ismail, a British citizen, found himself having to pay more for his flight to Cairo than his wife and children. This differential in ticket prices was based on more expensive tickets for people with 'foreign names'. His wife and children had English surnames. This case with Egypt Air resulted in the CRE sending letters to 78 airlines operating in the UK about the legality of differential prices based on ethnicity. British Airways has undertaken to stop the practice of checking passports and photocopying them for black British citizens but not white citizens. They have also had to stop the practice of refusing travel to black British citizens going to Europe on a one-way ticket (whilst allowing this for white Britons). Sudan Airways had an injunction taken out against them by the CRE for banning all Somali travellers from using their flights.

Insurance companies were found to be discriminating against minority ethnic customers by giving better terms to people who had been resident in the UK all their lives. Staff were told to ask callers about length of residency if they had 'ethnic sounding names'. Alliance Insurance Centres Ltd was one of the companies that operated differential underwriting criteria for customers who had not been resident in the UK all their lives. The court order agreed terms with the CRE which included a series of other insurance companies.

Mortgage companies have been liable under the SDA. For example, the Yorkshire Building Society in 1997 refused to take into account a woman's earnings because she was going on maternity leave, in spite of the fact that she intended to return to work.

Hotels have also been found liable for discrimination. Most recently (1997) a hotel in Derby agreed a settlement over a racial harassment case. This rested on the fact that a speaker at a function (Bernard Manning) and some customers racially abused two black members of staff. Employers are liable for subjecting an employee to racial harassment unless reasonable preventative measures have been taken. The same would apply to sexual harassment or harassment on the grounds of disability. The steps the hotel has taken will now be a model for the hospitality industry to follow. They include amending terms and conditions of hire for hospitality facilities requiring third parties to be responsible for their guests' behaviour; improving training to managers to make them more aware of their obligations to protect staff from harassment by customers; and procedures for managers to brief staff prior to events.

Pubs were found liable in 1988 for putting up signs which said 'No Travellers'. Gypsies who were targeted by this notice were deemed to be an ethnic group by the Court of Appeal. In 1992 the CRE investigated clubs and found that rules which made new members get proposers and seconders from within the existing membership could be indirectly discriminating on the grounds of race (if the existing membership was 'white'). As a result of this investigation model rules for club membership were changed. The CRE has now produced a publication covering pubs, clubs and recreational services called *Have You Been Served?* which outlines the cases which apply to these three categories of service providers. In 1992 a pub was found to discriminate on the grounds of sex when it adopted an admission policy under which men were not allowed to wear earrings whereas women were.

Organizations can, under certain circumstances, take customers to court if they are in breach of the Acts. For example, in 1996 Islington Council evicted a tenant whose 15-year-old son continually harassed local Bengali families. This was done using the Housing Act 1985 for breach of tenancy agreement. The tenancy agreement included an anti-harassment clause. Other councils are acting in similar ways by withdrawing services from customers who discriminate against other customers on racial grounds when there is a definite policy or contract which includes anti-harassment clauses. Following the ruling above concerning hotels, service providers other than local authorities should also include such clauses.

Discrimination on grounds other than gender, race and disability

There is at present no legislation in this country outlawing discrimination on the grounds of age or sexuality. People from these two groups are only protected in law if they fall into one of the groupings covered by the SDA, RRA and DDA. For example, an older man can use the SDA to get a service related to 'pensionable age' if this means women get the service at 60 and men at 65. However, there is legislation which allows for discrimination to take place. For instance, s. 28 of the Local Government Act 1988 says that a local authority 'shall not intentionally promote homosexuality or publish material with the intention of promoting homosexuality and shall not promote the teaching in any maintained school of the acceptability of homosexuality as a pretended family relationship'. This in effect has meant that local authorities and schools have used s. 28 to discriminate against lesbians and gay men by denying access to books and materials. Immigration rules have discriminated against lesbians and gay men in as much as there has been no provision for lesbians and gay men bringing their partners into the country. This is due to be changed in 1998.

The pensioners' movement has long campaigned for legislation making age discrimination illegal on the same grounds as the SDA and RRA. It seems likely that such legislation will be introduced in the near future, but it is unclear whether this will cover service delivery or just employment.

In terms of sexuality, the lesbian and gay movement are asking for 'equal citizenship – a society in which lesbians, gay men and bisexuals enjoy the same rights, respect and responsibility as heterosexuals' (Stonewall 1997). This would include recognition of same-sex couples who should be afforded the same rights as heterosexual couples; legislation should include equal parenting rights with the right to foster or adopt being judged on ability alone and not sexuality; same-sex parents should be recognized as legal parents; s. 28 must be repealed; and school bullying policies should be able to deal with homophobic violence and the needs of young lesbians and gay men. Once the European convention on Human Rights is incorporated into UK law, this will afford rights to all including lesbians and gay men and older people.

Other legal instruments which stress anti-discriminatory practices

There are laws which do not directly themselves relate to equalities but which have sections on equalities or implications for equalities.

The Children Act 1989 places a duty on local authorities in England and Wales to consider the racial and cultural needs of children looked after by the authority (s. 22(5)(c)). It states that 'due consideration to the child's religious persuasion, racial origin and cultural and linguistic background' must be given by social services departments. This applies to day care and fostering.

The NHS and Community Care Act 1990 recognizes that different ethnic groups have different needs and places an obligation on service providers to plan appropriate provision in consultation with those groups. The Act also requires consultation with disabled people and older people to assess their different needs.

To combat racism in football, the Football (Offences) Act was passed in 1991. This makes racist chanting unlawful:

> It is an offence to take part at a designated football match in chanting of an indecent or racialist nature.
>
> For this purpose – 'chanting' means the repeated uttering of any words or sounds in concert with one or more others; and 'of a racialist nature' means consisting of or including matter which is threatening, abusive or insulting to a person by reason of his colour, race, nationality (including citizenship) or ethnic or national origins.
>
> (s. 3(1) and (2)(*a*)(*b*))

The Protection from Harassment Act (1997) prohibits 'a course of conduct' which amounts to harassment and which the perpetrator 'knows or ought to know' amounts to harassment of another. The Act can be used for racial harassment cases (service delivery and employment). Victims can bring civil action and be granted injunctions against perpetrators.

The European Convention on Human Rights should be incorporated into UK law in 1998. The Convention covers the right to freedom from arbitrary arrest, freedom of thought, religion and association, and respect for privacy and family life. Once incorporated it will be enforceable through UK courts and tribunals.

Conclusion

This chapter reviewed current British legislation on equalities. Major deficiencies in British anti-discriminatory legislation are that discrimination on the grounds of sexuality and on the grounds of age are at present left out. Equivalent legislation in Ireland (the Irish Employment Equality Act) is much broader although it covers only employment and not service delivery. The Irish Act prohibits discrimination on grounds of gender, marital status, family status, sexual orientation, religious belief, age, disability, race and membership of the travelling community. There have been inconsistencies between different legal instruments in the UK: discrimination on the grounds of religion is outlawed in Northern Ireland but not in Britain. Within particular Acts there are inconsistencies with international law. In terms of the provision of services to the public, government bodies are only covered if they are performing similar functions to private sector bodies. This is inconsistent with international human rights law. As a result government services such as immigration and taxation are not covered by equalities legislation (see *Equal Opportunities Review* 1997). One deficiency in the powers accorded to the EOC and the CRE is that they cannot take 'class action'. They do not have the power to take cases on behalf of whole groups of people. Each individual has to take their own case.

The Amsterdam Treaty negotiated by the Council of Ministers in 1997 has a clause outlawing discrimination. Article 6a states: 'the Council . . . may take appropriate action to combat discrimination based on sex, racial or ethnic origin, religion or belief, disability, age or sexual orientation.' This is unlikely to be particularly effective as any legal measures derived from Article 6a must be adopted unanimously by the Council rather than on a single majority vote.

There are international human rights treatises, to which the UK is a signatory, which have anti-discriminatory articles. For these redress can be obtained in the International Court at The Hague but the process is extremely lengthy. The International Covenant on Civic and Political Rights (Article 26) states that 'the law shall prohibit any discrimination and guarantee to all persons equal and effective protection against discrimination on any grounds such as race, colour, sex, language, religion, political or other opinion, national or social origin, property, birth or other status'. As yet, language, political or other opinion, property, birth or other status are not covered by UK law. Within Article 26 'sex' covers sexuality which is not the case under the SDA.

Legislation provides the minimum equalities standards within which service providers must operate. Legislation does not, however, enable providers to know which services might discriminate and which might not. In order to be able to tell which services are the most appropriate for different groups of people, it is necessary to ask the different groups of people themselves. The next chapter is about assessing different people's needs and explains how different forms of consultation can be used to achieve this.

4

IDENTIFYING NEEDS:
INVOLVING THE PUBLIC

The previous chapter summarized the legal requirements for organizations delivering services to the public. These place clear obligations on service providers not to discriminate. But how is an organization to know when it is discriminating? It isn't enough to wait for complaints. Complaints can pinpoint discrimination but are an inefficient method of finding out if services are accessible to all. As said in Chapter 2, discrimination can occur when the needs of some groups of people are not being met. The best way to find out what people need is to ask them. This provides the key to 'move from provider- to user-led services, match services to people instead of forcing people to fit into services, start with human instead of organisational issues' (Beresford and Croft 1993: 111). People themselves have expert knowledge on what they require from a service or what they see as fair for them. This is true even if people are not always very good at expressing their views: 'our judgement may not be perfect, but it is difficult to argue that we are not the primary judges of our needs and wants' (Prior, Stewart and Walsh 1995: 64). In public services, providers have traditionally turned to professionals to provide advice. Professionals know a great deal but the true experts on women's needs are women, the true experts on the needs of black and minority ethnic people are black people themselves, the experts on age are older people, the experts on disability, disabled people and the experts on lesbian and gay issues are lesbians and gay men. Consultation or some form of public involvement is crucial to ensure that services are appropriate and do not discriminate.

The following example illustrates how providing a service without proper consultation can be a waste of resources. A police station in West London was not accessible to wheelchair users so it installed an alarm at the bottom of the steps leading up to the station. However, no one asked wheelchair users if this was useful. As it turned out the alarm bell was too high to be reached by someone sitting in a wheelchair. Consultation is crucial to provide more effective targeting. Redesigning services on the basis of consultation with the public is not new. The GLC, for example, undertook wide consultation with women in London in the early 1980s where policy makers listened to women's voices (see GLC 1986b: 7). The exercise involved asking different groups of women about their needs: black and minority ethnic women, older women, lesbians and disabled women. The findings influenced policy on housing, transport, safety and design for open spaces. Since that time more and more organizations have seen the advantage of consulting the public.

There has been, since the late eighties, a growing realization that the public should be involved both in the management of services and the design of services. This goes one step further than mere consultation where an organization takes soundings of people's views but retains the complete power to make decisions. It signifies a move towards public participation in the decision-making process whereby the service provider works in partnership with the community. This trend, towards organizations listening and learning from their customers and getting closer to the service user in order to steer services forward, is now being embraced by many service providers. Delivering services in partnership *with* the public rather than delivering services simply *to* the public is a more efficient means of service delivery. In spite of this trend, many organizations still feel that they know best and do not see the need for consultation let alone greater involvement. Indeed, some fear consultation because people might tell them things they do not want to hear. For example, many health authorities which have been urged by the Department of Health to set up listening panels since 1992 had still not done so by 1995 according to a survey by the University of Leeds (Donaldson 1995).

This chapter will first look at why public involvement is important for fair and efficient service delivery, then examine what the different forms of public involvement are, consider how to consult different groups in the community and finally give an analysis of the pitfalls that are likely to confront anyone undertaking public involvement. In writing this chapter I have made extensive use of guidance notes from the London Borough of Hounslow (1994a) and the London Borough of Croydon (1997b).

Why involve the public?

The Association of Metropolitan Authorities (AMA, now the Local Government Association (LGA)) said that public involvement had five purposes: 'to give information, to get feedback, to allow comment, to bring in new ideas and to create consensus where possible' (AMA 1993: 99). All these contribute to improving services by identifying need. An experiment was conducted in Croydon in 1995 with this in mind (Moore 1995a). One hundred and fifty people were invited for a two-day experiment in tailoring community care services to need. The event was organized by the local authority and the health authority. This event took six months to plan and brought together a careful mix of people in terms of cultural background and age. Those invited included staff from both authorities, a postman, someone from the gas board, a police officer and elderly residents. The main outcome was that people wanted a greater choice of services tailored to individual needs. The detail of people's requirements was fed back into the Community Care Plan. The event allowed people to speak for themselves rather than being told what to say or do.

Consultation is not easy but worth it if services become more efficient and effective. It is also a way of showing service users that they are valued.

In local authorities, councillors often feel that they are elected to represent the views of their constituents and therefore do not need to involve the public. They feel that somehow public involvement will threaten representative democracy. This is a mistaken view. As John Stewart points out: 'the more citizens participate the stronger is the elected representative because he or she is then better informed by the views of those represented . . . In the end the councillor has to bring a political judgement to bear on the representations made. It will be a better judgement if informed by citizens' views in all their diversity' (1995: 2). This is about accountability. Accountability means that everyone should 'count' when decisions are being made; this can only be achieved through public involvement. In cases where those who are making decisions are not typically representative of the public or their service users, public involvement is all the more important. Involving the public also makes it possible to test ideas out before they are put into practice and thus avoid errors. Bradford Council has a 'Speak Out' panel where citizens can air their views; it 'helps tune public ears more sensitively to issues before they reach boiling point' (Donaldson 1995). Being involved and having a say is a democratic right.

Public involvement is a means of communicating with service users which improves service delivery. In a publication about information to patients the Audit Commission comments: 'there is a growing body of evidence to show that if providers improve communication they can in turn improve the effectiveness of care, increase the efficiency with which it is delivered, and improve their reputation locally with both patients and purchasers' (Audit Commission 1993: 1). By consulting with service users, providers will ensure that decisions are more easily implemented because users will understand why this is being done and to some extent accept and own the outcome. For example, when Milton Keynes Council needed to restructure it embarked on a public involvement exercise: 'Rather than attempt to persuade that community to support the council's viewpoint, we felt Milton Keynes would be in a more powerful position if the council adopted the local population's wishes' (Morris 1995). In opening a new supermarket, a company could benefit from consulting the local community to find out special requirements, particularly in relation to the minority ethnic population. This could draw in new groups of customers.

Different forms of public involvement

There are different forms of public involvement. Some is simply information giving, some is information gathering (consultation) and some involves the public in participating in the decision-making process. Each will be appropriate for different uses depending on the aim of the exercise. There is a continuum between information, consultation and participation. On the whole information giving offers less involvement from the public than consultation and participation offers more involvement than consultation. It helps to be clear about which form of public involvement to choose and it helps to be clear with the public which approach is being taken. The difference between them is well illustrated by the following examples from *Going Public* (London Borough of Hounslow 1994a). In a luncheon club for older people an exercise on the timing of lunch could be simple information giving: 'Lunch will be served at 12.30 prompt.' This is a one-way process. Or it could be genuine consultation: 'Lunch will be served at 12.30. Is that OK with you?' This is a two-way process involving a dialogue with the users. Or it could be participation: 'What time do you want lunch or do you want lunch to be provided?' This empowers users to be involved in the decision-making process. Participation is closest to the notion of citizen as given in the introduction to this book, in which the citizen has rights. It is a democratic approach: 'Among politicians, academics, researchers and others there has been, during the 1990s, growing interest in the way experiments with participation and empowerment at the local, neighbourhood, level can be linked to the broader context of discussions about citizenship and the regeneration of local democracy' (Department of the Environment 1995: 7). Information giving and consultation are closer to a consumer model of citizenship. Whichever is chosen will be more effective if it is part of a continuing programme of public involvement. Each form of involvement will now be examined in more detail.

Information

Information giving should be used if there is a legal requirement to do so, if it is the company's policy to inform, or if the organization wishes the public to know about something. In giving information to the public use plain, jargon-free English. Information is more effective if the message is kept relevant, attractive, short and simple. Beresford and Croft advise asking the following questions before giving information:

- Who are we trying to reach?
- Whose language are we using?
- What information do people need?
- When will they want it?
- Where can it be provided most helpfully?
- What forms will be most effective?
- What support will people need to make the best use of it?

(1993: 65)

To this list should be added the need to identify resources to carry out the exercise and to ensure that adequate time is allowed to complete it.

Consultation

As with information giving, consultation should be used if there is a legal requirement to do so, if the organization wants to know the views of its users and if there is a policy to consult. Beresford and Croft (1993) list the following aims of any consultation exercise: to find out what people think of the service; whether they know about it; whether people's experience of the service is different for different groups of people; whether they know how to get and use the service; whether all users are treated equally. In improving their services providers can learn to change the service, prioritize, evaluate their performance and improve their image. As Beresford and Croft say, 'We only have to remind ourselves of commercial slogans like "the listening bank", "a business inspired by its consumers", and "it's you we answer to", to appreciate the importance invested in consultation' (1993: 27). One example of a successful consultation exercise is described by Bywaters and McLeod (1996: 60–1): consultation meetings on head lice were organized between a group of women and the local Community Health Council. The outcome of the meeting was that myths about head lice were prevalent in the community, that the roles of teachers, nurses and parents were unclear, that no local clinics provided lotions and that the health authority leaflet was difficult to understand. The result was a series of changes addressing the issues which had been identified. For consultation to be useful, it is important to ensure that the public have all the information they need, that there is a clear mechanism for dealing with contributions and the way in which these will be fed back to decision makers. For example, in the Hounslow case mentioned above, if the service users are not happy with lunch being served at 12.30, the providers could be asked to change the current arrangements. As with information, resources and timescales for completing the exercise need to be identified. Consultation is more controlled by the agency and more concerned with the agency's needs than participation. And as Beresford and Croft say, 'this can limit people's willingness to get involved, qualify the development of their opinions and inhibit the expression of their views' (1993: 47).

Participation

Participation signifies a particular commitment to share decision making with the public on a specific issue. This is a process of empowerment: 'Empowerment is about increasing the power of the public in relation to the institutions and organisations whose activities affect their way of life. By power we mean the extent of influence and control exercised over such activities' (Prior, Stewart and Walsh 1995: 81). An organization may want the public to be involved in the day-to-day running of a service, setting standards for services, monitoring complaints, staff selection, identifying priorities, planning or reviewing a service. The difference between consultation and participation is that with the latter there is a greater commitment to share decision making. Participation is about genuine partnership, if still limited, with the community. How much power will be given to the public needs to be carefully worked out and the whole exercise carefully planned: 'Partnerships need therefore to develop their strategic objectives and priorities first. Only then should they seek to develop project ideas' (Department of the Environment 1994: 5). According to Beresford and Croft the following should be considered:

- clarify what kind of involvement is on offer
- involve people from the start
- make clear the limits of involvement

- provide safeguards for involvement
- set small but attainable goals for change
- build in involvement as part of the agency structure and process
- establish a continuing process of involvement
- make specific provision for the involvement of minority ethnic communities
- develop appropriate forms and forums
- allow people's involvement to be flexible and open-ended
- ensure involvement is by choice, not compulsion
- involve all the key participants concerned
- give priority to people's own accounts of their wants and needs.

(1993: 93)

The community may be involved in work in between meetings (designing questionnaires, conducting interviews), or be involved in setting the agenda for any participative event. In one example in Devon, users were involved in the training of health service managers. Those helping with the training were part of a panel of eight users who acted as advisers to NHS managers: 'The panel includes two people with multiple sclerosis, two with physical disabilities, one mental health patient and two carers of children with severe disabilities. The aim is to both make training more relevant to everyday issues and help managers see services from the users' perspective' (Moore 1995b). Participation can involve individuals or groups. Different methods can be used such as meetings, joint working groups, co-opting members of the public onto a decision-making body within the organization. The principles which apply to consultation also apply to participation. Participation will be useful where there appears to be a good chance of reaching a consensus or of resolving conflict. If participation is to be effective, people will need support and skills to take part. There are barriers to people feeling comfortable with participation, which need to be removed if the exercise is to be successful. Barriers may be related to the need for information, or practical support such as childcare, transport, training and interpreters. Engaging in participation will usually mean a culture change for the organization. Participation isn't just about training users to be part of the 'professionals'; 'the onus for change is mainly on the service provider' (Beresford and Croft 1993: 21). As one provider said: 'I've had to learn to work in a different way. I've learned to ask rather than tell. In one way it's easier to make decisions behind people's back' (quoted in Beresford and Croft 1993: 51).

Methods of public involvement

The whole process of public involvement needs careful thought. Consideration should be given to issues such as who will be involved, what status the information given by the public will have, how this will be monitored and how the exercise will be explained to the public. A successful exercise will usually build on what people already understand. Key principles are to 'listen to what people say', 'keep people informed', 'offer support and direction', 'enable reciprocity and exchange with a two way traffic of understanding and experience' (see Beresford and Croft 1993: 160–3). This does not mean that there will not be conflict. For example, families and children may be included in a case conference about the future of a child and the decision may not be the one they want. However, the decision will be a better one for being informed by the families' views. For involvement to be successful, it is important to be clear about the exercise (information, consultation or participation) and what it will be used for. The parameters of the exercise should be clearly laid down and communicated so that false hopes are not raised. It should be linked to other policy processes to ensure good use of the results. Which method to choose will depend on what is wanted from the exercise. The next section goes through the options. Public involvement will only be meaningful if there is a representative sample of the public, but this will vary depending on the community chosen for the exercise (locality or community of interest). Ensuring this is the topic of a further section of this chapter. Finally, reporting back to the public on outcomes is important as it shows the organization is to some extent accountable for its decision to those who helped in the decision-making process.

Before deciding which method to use it is important to:

- Clarify the aims of the exercise (what is the desired outcome?).
- Select the constituency to be consulted; this could be a geographical locality or a particular group of people.
- Define the type of service to be studied and the nature of the data to be collected. The service may be delivered at someone's home (meals on wheels) or an open place (market); it may be voluntarily chosen (sport) or imposed (prison).
- Determine whether information sought needs to be statistical or analytical. In the first case quantitative methods will be more appropriate, in the second qualitative methods will give more insight. Qualitative information allows for the exploration of people's attitudes. It may be that a mixture of both is the most useful.
- Assess how participative the exercise should be, whether it should be part of a longer exercise and how open the agenda will be.

Answers to these will help show whether a single exercise (e.g. postal questionnaire) or a continuous one (e.g. user group) will be more useful. It may be that a whole series of methods should be included. This was the approach Milton Keynes District Council took when it embarked on a public involvement exercise on its structure. A questionnaire was used; a series of seminars were run looking at different aspects of council work; special interest focus groups were organized for older people, disabled people, the business community and others; a large panel of 500 residents was established to be representative of the population and interviewed; and a one-day event was organized with workshops involving 250 people (see Morris 1995). In this way Milton Keynes was able to get 'the informed views of ordinary citizens' (Stewart 1995: 3). All the information gathered was taken into account in decisions to restructure the council.

Complaints

A complaints system offers a good source of information as well as a mechanism for holding service providers to account. Indeed complaints about a service should be incorporated into every public involvement exercise, and seen as complimentary to comment card systems and suggestion boxes. In large organizations it helps to make a named person responsible for dealing with complaints. When making a complaint, people should also have the chance to comment generally. Often people do not complain because they believe it is a waste of time as nothing will be done, or they fear reprisals from the service provider. Not obtaining complaints is a waste of resources as a well-organized complaints system is invaluable, not only for bringing issues to the attention of the organization, but also as it can resolve minor problems informally. Complaints methods should:

- be well publicized, so that people know about them
- be clearly set out, so they can be understood
- be accessible
- be independent and include the right of external appeal, to ensure fair and proper treatment
- offer independent advocacy, to help people frame and pursue their complaints
- be rapid, with fixed time limits
- be regularly monitored as a basis for improving practice and services
- have their recommendations accepted by agencies.

(Beresford and Croft 1993: 166)

Information giving methods

Organizations have numerous ways of providing information, all with advantages and disadvantages. Information can be delivered *directly* through letters and written information or by personal contact (personal visits or telephone contact). It can also be given *indirectly* by distribution of leaflets, news releases and exhibitions. The advantage of direct information is that it can target those the organization wishes to reach. Personal contact also has the advantage that issues can be clarified by users asking questions. The disadvantages of direct provision of information are that it relies on accurate information on the whereabouts of users, and direct provision becomes more expensive as the number of users increases. Moreover, the use of written information could exclude people who are blind, do not read English or are illiterate. When using leaflets the advantage of the method is that it can reach large numbers of people at relatively little cost. A disadvantage is that the leaflets may not reach those who use the service, and if left lying about can go out of date. News releases are useful but only if the media use them – the disadvantage is that this is not guaranteed; moreover the information may be changed by the editor. Exhibitions, which can be temporary, permanent, stationary or mobile, are also effective. They require resources, particularly if the exhibition is staffed. However, they only provide information to those who visit the exhibition.

Consultation methods

Consultation can be carried out by sending written information (policy statements, proposals for change) to individuals or groups and requesting comments; by face-to-face interviews with selected representatives; by sending out self-completion questionnaires; by telephone interviews; by holding public meetings or conferences; and by running focus groups or discussion groups with selected representatives. Consultation can take place at the point of service delivery, in a person's home or a public meeting place. Sending out documents for comments can be expensive; it relies on people being motivated; it may only get responses from 'professionals'; and will exclude people who cannot read. Face-to-face interviews are also expensive as they are time-consuming and require trained staff, but with a well-chosen sample they can provide useful data, although sometimes answers vary so much as to be difficult to analyse. Self-completion questionnaires can be cheap, anonymous and easy to analyse but people may not complete them, particularly if they are long or complicated; they exclude those who cannot read. Telephone interviews are quick, but they exclude those who do not have a telephone, who refuse to answer or find the exercise intrusive. In general, for all the above methods, people are put off by questions that are long.

Public meetings provide another method of consultation, and these have the advantage that issues can be clearly explained and different views heard. People have a chance to test and form their judgement in the light of other people's views. The main disadvantage of public meetings is that they only attract those who like going to public meetings; they are therefore unlikely to be representative. In addition many who attend do not contribute as they find public meetings are bureaucratic and intimidating. Public meetings are often put on to discuss issues that interest the organizing body more than the public. If this is also felt by the public such meetings will not be popular as people will feel that the agency has already made up its mind and that the meeting is just a public relations exercise. It is best to be clear about the parameters of the meeting, its limits and possible outcomes. When they are of interest to the public (road closures, town centre developments) such meetings are often confrontational, with a platform of 'experts' facing the public. These are unlikely to lead to a constructive exchange of views. It is better in such cases to break a public meeting up into smaller groups where discussion can take place in a less adversarial manner. The overall aim of a public meeting designed for consultation, must be:

- to provide information to the public
- to seek views, preferences, or ideas from the public
- to encourage interaction between groups
- to obtain agreements on ways of dealing with issues.

                              (Creighton 1994, quoted by Stewart 1995: 24)

Public hearings are another form of consultation. They provide a chance to hear public views as well as the views of experts. They are useful for exploring issues in depth. The evidence received is submitted to the organizing body for decision.

Focus and discussion groups allow representative participation, are more informal than public meetings and offer the opportunity of being more creative. Issues can be discussed in greater depth. Examples could be a two-day workshop looking into a specific service from the point of view of the users, or half days with selected representatives of the public testing out their views on a range of services. The disadvantages of focus groups and discussion groups are that discussion can wander off the real agenda; they can be dominated by one or two articulate members; some people might find it difficult to express their views if these differ from others in the group; and it can be very difficult to quantify the outcome. One group frequently not consulted but who often have knowledge of what customers want are members of staff. They should be included in any consultation exercise and their views should be sought on how to improve the service. Front-line staff often live in the locality and for this reason too are aware of the views of the local community.

Participation methods

User groups who themselves manage the service they receive (as opposed to merely being consulted on it), although still pretty rare, are probably the most common form of participation. User groups exist in leisure centres and housing estates. User groups can manage budgets as well as recruit and select staff. Sometimes a user group will be part of a joint management committee whereby the service is jointly managed by users and staff.

In local authorities, area committees which have power devolved to them from the Town Hall offer a participative mechanism. Birmingham City Council has area committees which consider council issues affecting the area. Neighbourhood forums and advisory bodies play a similar role; they are usually made up of elected local representatives and have a right to be consulted on issues of concern. Some forums can be service specific, for example Social Security Consultative Committees, based around a local Benefits Agency Office and including users (claimants), members of organizations which represent users and social security staff. They consider service development and improvement.

Other participative mechanisms include citizens' panels which are formed as a basis for carrying out opinion surveys. They can comprise up to 2,000 people but usually consist of only 100 to 200 people representing the larger community. A panel will be used as a sounding board for new ideas and to comment on existing services giving an informed view. The panel may meet monthly and could have a regular change of 10 per cent of its membership at each meeting. A citizens' panel can be permanent or established to do a particular piece of research. Kirklees Council and the West Yorkshire Health Authority have set up a joint panel called 'Talk Back' with 1,000 local people. This was launched in May 1995. The panel is designed to give feedback on the way services are run and should be run. The organizers claim that the panel is more cost-effective than conducting full-scale surveys to sample public views on services. John Harman, who was the leader of Kirklees Council in 1995, saw the panel as a management tool rather than a political tool (Donaldson 1995).

Study circles consist of a group of people who meet on three or more occasions and discuss a particular issue with a volunteer facilitator. They can be built around existing networks such as religious or neighbourhood groups. Those attending can be offered a small fee.

A citizens' jury provides an enquiry of greater depth than can be offered by a study circle. In a citizens' jury a group of 12 to 22 citizens explore a policy issue or a specific decision to be made. They are given the power to call witnesses and to ask for specific documents. They then deliberate. A trained moderator facilitates the proceedings which can last up to a week. The moderator gives the final report which will include the views of the jury, any weighting attached to different views and the reasons for this and recommendations. Lewisham Council in London ran a citizens' jury in 1996 looking at what could be done to reduce harm to the community and to individuals from abuse of drugs. A market research company and consultants were hired to select the jury and facilitate proceedings; there were 16 jurors selected as a representative sample of Lewisham's population. The jury met over four days and two evenings. The questions to be discussed were decided after several focus group meetings. The jury had a say in the agenda and decided on which drugs should be looked at. They heard evidence from the police, drug users, community safety workers, a consultant psychologist and primary and secondary school head teachers. A full report of their findings was delivered to the council. The whole process from setting up the jury to delivery of the report took six months. Citizens' juries are expensive to run as jurors and moderators need to be paid for their time.

A future search is another participative method where a group of eight or ten 'stakeholders' are chosen to plan an event, including the reason for the search and how it will be run. Twelve to sixty-four representative individuals are then invited to a two- or three-day event where the past is reviewed, the present mapped out and plans for the future proposed. Action plans are then drawn up by the 'stakeholders'. Richmond Council did this in conjunction with Rail-track in 1996 to plan a new railway station. This process is similar to 'planning for real' where those involved are given models of plans under discussion and cards suggesting different usages and different problems. The cards are meant to facilitate discussion.

Equalities issues

Inequality is a cause of social exclusion, where some groups of people feel they do not belong to an area or a particular community. Those who feel excluded from society see no point in being consulted or in participating in planning the delivery of any service. Only when people feel that their rights as human beings are recognized and that they are being treated with respect will they be willing to become involved. Unless people's needs are considered and they are 'equipped to participate, participatory initiatives are likely to mirror or *perpetuate* prevailing race, gender, class and other inequalities instead of challenging them' (Beresford and Croft 1993: 52). Indeed mechanisms such as user groups can become little cliques – for example all-white, excluding black and minority ethnic people. Involving people can perpetuate discrimination. But involvement can also be a powerful tool to combat discrimination. All the involvement mechanisms outlined above, from information to participation, can be used to redress the balance. They can be used to find out the views and needs of the largely invisible majority of the population.

To ensure that all views are considered when consulting the public, it is important to start by considering whether someone's membership of a particular group (e.g. black and minority ethnic, older, disabled) will affect their ability to get involved. If established groups are being consulted check that they adequately reflect the community they represent.

Information should take into account the needs of different groups such as:

- Linguistic and cultural needs (ensure clear English, culturally appropriate messages and possibly different languages). During the Association of London Authorities (ALA) Zero Tolerance campaign one poster had in English a caption stating, 'he gave her flowers, chocolates and multiple bruises.' This was translated literally into other languages. The message was lost to those communities where men do not give 'chocolates'. One authority failed to communicate its message on International Women's Day by mistakenly including, for a number of years, 'Come and celebrate International Day of Women Wrestlers' in the Gujarati translation on the poster.
- Those with sensory disabilities (provide large print, Braille or tape, signers at public meetings).
- People with limited mobility (ensure displays are not too high and are at accessible venues).
- People with limited literacy (ensure material is in plain English). It also helps to link verbal and written information and to offer people the chance to discuss the information given to them with a service provider: 'the most successful way of contacting people was by literally going out and speaking to them face to face' (Beresford and Croft 1993: 35).

Ultimately it may only be by reaching out to different communities that information gets across. Camden Council has pioneered the use of a videophone information service allowing people to communicate with the council in sign language via linked television screens in its public libraries (see ALG 1997a: 13).

Consultation planning needs to take into account issues such as:

- Timing: meetings in the evening will not attract women, parents of small children, older people. It is impossible to find a time which is right for all. If you need to attract a mixed group of people it is better to have a meeting in the daytime on a Saturday and provide childcare. It is also important to avoid consulting on religious festivals which would exclude a particular section of the population. A public meeting should not be held on Diwali, for example, in an area with a Hindu community.
- Location: meetings held near to where people are or where people usually meet are bound to be more successful and are a way of ensuring better representation of disadvantaged groups. If a consultation is set up in a mother and toddler club, this will increase the likelihood of obtaining the

views of mothers and carers; a public meeting elsewhere would be unlikely to be successful. If public meetings are held, it is best to hold them in venues people use for other purposes: schools, libraries, clinics. But more will be learned by visiting groups themselves. For example: 'When one local authority tried to consult women through public meetings, it discovered it was only reaching those who identified themselves as feminist. So contact was made with a wide range of women's organisations, including traditional civic groups, an Indian women's group, girls' and disabled women's groups, enabling a much broader spectrum of women to be heard. As a result, the women's officer concluded, "it was not possible for management to hide behind the belief that it is only a small number of feminist or middle class women who want changes in the way council services operate"' (Beresford and Croft 1993: 37). For women, older people or disabled people it is always better to go to where they are rather than expect them to come to where it is convenient to the organization.

- Buildings: these need to be accessible for those with limited mobility (disabled people, older people, parents with small children). This means providing ramps but also doors which open easily, lifts to floors which may be used and toilets for disabled people. Venues also need to be inviting and friendly: 'the unspoken messages . . . the sights, sounds, cultural and spacial cues, that tell us whether we are welcome and want to be somewhere' (Beresford and Croft 1993: 75). For example, the town halls where many public meetings are held often have a series of portraits of important past citizens (mainly past mayors). They are usually all white men. This sends a particularly uninviting message to some members of the community: this is not a welcome place for women or for black and minority ethnic people. As one resident said to me, 'It is as if the white men are clearly saying: "you do not belong here"'. Local authorities are not unusual in this respect; many organizations have portraits of 'important' figures in their lobbies and invariably these tend to be white men. People are more likely to come to a meeting in a building they see as theirs. The formality of many buildings puts people off.
- Language: provide interpreters for those who do not speak English, signers and induction loops for those with impaired hearing, an advocate for those with learning disabilities.
- Other needs: always consider the needs of those with children by providing a crèche (there are regulations governing the care of children check with the social services department of the local council) and transport for those who cannot get to the venue by public transport (disabled people and older people).
- Advertising: the way in which the meeting is advertised is important. This may need translated information and must indicate help available (transport, crèche, interpreters, signers). All these will make it clear that everybody is welcome. Bear in mind that the information is not accessible to those who are blind or have visual impairment. A local talking newspaper could be used.
- Running the meeting: if all the speakers at a public meeting are white able-bodied men, it won't encourage women, black and minority ethnic people

or disabled people to feel that the meeting concerns them. When conducting the meeting, if several people are allowed to speak at once, those with impaired hearing will not be able to hear and signers will have difficulty interpreting. The same applies to people who speak very fast. Make sure different people have a chance to speak. Those who are not used to speaking in public will need encouragement. Experience shows that if women are not allowed to speak in the first few minutes of a meeting, few women will speak at all. Try to get a mixture of contributors right from the start.

There are cost implications to much of the above, but without these the consultation exercise could be ineffective and meaningless.

Participation represents the most powerful mechanism for ensuring that the views of all are heard. Facilitating service users to give their perspective on the service is invaluable. For example, groups of people who face specific disadvantage in relation to a particular service can be helped to form an advocacy group 'designed to redress inequality in power within a locality by helping groups and individuals challenge assumptions, define and fight for their rights, influence decisions and, thereby, secure services that better meet their requirements' (Weaver 1996: 104). In the 1980s when work of this kind was done with women, findings showed that many women find it difficult to formulate their ideas in terms of 'demand statements like "I want" or "we need" ' (Beresford and Croft 1993: 132). Forming advocacy groups can help with this process. This is also empowering for a group of clients with learning disabilities or a group with a particular cultural identity (e.g. Turkish Cypriots). The following is an example quoted by Stewart (1995: 18): 'When Stockport Social Services Department decided to give physically handicapped people, the parents of mentally handicapped people and elderly people a decisive say in how their clubs and centres were run and how their budgets were spent, the initial decisions were different from those that would have been made by the authority. Chairs, tables and curtains were bought, for example, which were not what the local authority would have purchased.'

Generally, in order to reach particular groups of people consider the following:

- Black and minority ethnic communities: people may not be organized in the standard local groups (e.g. residents' associations) so approach specialist groups representing black and minority interests. English may not be the first language, so provide information in other languages. Cultural and religious practices may influence who gets involved (men and women may not be able to meet together), avoid meeting on religious festivals, offer separate meetings. Minority ethnic communities are diverse, so respect the diversity and aim to meet different needs (e.g. Asian women may need to be consulted separately).
- Women: caring responsibilities often limit women's ability to get involved, so make information available at places women attend (schools, clinics), provide crèches and transport and hold meetings locally. Women often do not participate verbally in meetings; this can be overcome by breaking the meeting up into workshops and by a good chair who will bring women into

the discussion. Women may feel unsafe going out at night, so organize meetings in daylight hours.

- Lesbians and gay men: it may be difficult for them to be open about their sexuality and their needs. If appropriate organize separate meetings or meet with local lesbian and gay groups. Ensure that information is circulated through local or national networks.
- Disabled people: one of the main barriers to involvement can be the attitude of service providers. Ensure that those conducting consultation understand the social model of disability (see Chapter 2). It may be necessary to provide separate meetings. Instead of providing information through carers, provide it directly to service users using large print, Braille, tapes. Ensure that organizations representing disabled people are run by disabled people themselves rather than charitable organizations run on behalf of disabled people which may not represent their views. Do not assume that all disabled people are the same or have similar views. It may be important to record different views or even hold separate meetings for people with different forms of disability.
- Older people: older people face barriers to involvement in similar ways to disabled people – the barrier is often the attitude of those undertaking the consultation exercise. Older people get labelled as frail and confused and so denied a say. Consult groups which have significant numbers of older people and groups specifically for older people (e.g. pensioners' groups). But bear in mind that approximately 90 per cent of older people do not belong to pensioners' groups. Some older people cannot get out to a public meeting, so hold meetings where people live and meet (luncheon clubs, residential homes, local community centres, churches). Fear of attack will mean that many older people, particularly women, will not go out at night. Provide daytime meetings and transport to and from the venue.
- Other groups: children and young people are often left out of consultation exercises; they can be consulted through schools, youth clubs, on estates or in places where young people gather (outside a shopping centre, a station, in a park). Travellers, refugees, people with HIV/Aids are other groups often overlooked. They may need to be consulted in their groups (if they have any) or have special meetings arranged for them.

Problems and ways of overcoming them

Involving the public will not necessarily yield information on people's needs. But the results are more likely to be useful if the approaches are carefully planned and executed. It is equally important to ensure that the process is as smooth as possible. Public involvement brings with it numerous problems. This section looks at evaluation and overcoming problems.

Commitment to outcomes

There is no point in embarking on a public involvement exercise if the organization has no commitment to act on the outcome. If either senior managers, or front-line staff, or even customers, are not committed to the outcome, taking action upon the results will be more difficult. A public involvement exercise is likely to be more successful if there is no hidden agenda. Success is also more likely if those undertaking the exercise believe in people's ability to be involved and give meaningful information. Many 'professionals' still believe that the public are not capable of identifying their own needs or are unable to represent the views of other users. Their account-ability gets questioned: 'Who gives them the right to speak on behalf of others?' The argument that people are unrepresentative is commonly used by those who have no commitment to involving the public. These views are clear in a comment by a participant with learning disabilities: 'The initial objection to us taking part was that we hadn't got the skills. Then we got involved and spoke up and they said we were unrepresentative. We hadn't really got learning difficulties. We weren't typical of disabled people. Or they'd say someone put us up to it! They just couldn't believe we can speak for ourselves' (Beresford and Croft 1993: 18). This is a common feeling amongst community representatives. Another community representative commented: 'If they like what you say then they tell everyone they consulted people. If they don't, it was only a few people and not representative' (Beresford and Croft 1993: 44). Representativeness can be an issue if people are speaking on someone else's behalf but if they are speaking for themselves in a consultation exercise where they may be seen as representative (with the word used as an adjective, not a noun) of people like themselves it should not be an issue: 'Your validity may be your experience, for example of disability, or of using a particular service. You speak for yourself. No, you can't represent all disabled people, but you can speak from your experience' (Beresford and Croft 1993: 150). If people are speaking on behalf of others, as for example in a tenants' association, then a minimum standard of accountability and democracy is important. Any public involvement will need to take account of this if it is to be seen to be legitimate (for more information on this area see 'Issues of Legitimacy' in AMA 1993: 97).

Problems also arise when the organization has a lack of commitment, as might occur when public involvement is sought for the sake of it rather than for any real intention of acting on results. The public may experience 'infor-mation overload' or 'consultation fatigue' where they have been involved so many times with nothing to show for it. This occurred, for example, in the 1980s on the White City Estate near Shepherd's Bush in London. The estate had been the subject of many studies and much research without any improvements ever being made to people's daily lives. The results of the exercises were not reported back to the residents and no visible changes occurred on the estate. When BBC Television moved its premises to the area, offering the chance of money to be spent on the estate through the council (as a planning gain), it was extremely difficult to get any commitment from the residents to take part in consultation exercises. No one was keen to be con-sulted yet again, even when a considerable amount of money was on offer, because no one had any trust left in the local authority. People feel 'used' by endless involvement exercises resulting in no benefit to themselves. This can also happen when the same residents are used again and again in consultation exercises. They too can experience 'consultation fatigue', even if action does

follow. Some people feel that all they want is 'decent services' and not consultation. Sometimes it is better just to provide the service if it becomes
apparent that this is so. The problem is that often we need to consult to find
out what counts as 'decent services'. Whether services can be efficient without
the involvement of the public is debatable. Reporting back to those who have
been involved shows commitment. To do so the organization needs to ensure
that a list of those participating is kept. Reporting back is also important in
terms of accountability. In one sense or another all service providers are
accountable to their users (see Chapter 1). Outcomes should be reported back
to contributors, to the wider public, to policy makers and to staff who will be
involved in any implementation of the findings.

Evaluation

In evaluation the whole process should be looked at. A poor outcome would,
for example, result from an exercise where the aims and objectives had not
been defined in advance. Everyone involved might have expectations of the
results but the outcome must be discussed and agreed by all at the onset. If
front-line staff or members of the public have been involved in designing the
exercise, they also need to be told of the expectations: 'If a local authority gives
recognition to a network, or spends time and resources on consulting with a
forum, it has an obligation to make its own expectations as clear as possible,
not only to prevent confusion or misunderstanding, but to ensure the exercise
is effective' (AMA 1993: 101). The amount of confidence people have in the
exercise will affect the outcome: 'I don't like the day centre but I'm hardly
going to say it's no good, when they can use that to close it instead of
providing something we want' (Beresford and Croft 1993: 47). How the results
will be fed back into the decision-making process also needs to be thought
through. Frustration is bound to occur where a public involvement exercise
itself had not been well constructed. For example, if a questionnaire is being
used but the print size is small; or the design poor with bad layout; or the
questions are badly put (for example closed questions requiring only a yes/no
answer where graded answers were really needed); or questions are ambiguous;
or the questionnaire was badly structured; or even if a questionnaire was not
the appropriate method to find out the information required, then the outcome will be in jeopardy. The Audit Commission (1993: 46–7) makes these
points and gives the following as an example of irrelevant questions: in a
health service survey asking patients about the hotel services, waiting times
and information given at a local hospital but not asking them about the health
care received. Benchmarking is equally important for future evaluation; you
need to be able to compare results from one exercise to another. Part of any
evaluation should include indicators which would act as a measure of the
results: for example in sending out 100 questionnaires, set a target of how
many you expect back. This would be decided on the basis of the quantity of
answers likely to be received, the numbers which would be considered meaningful and whether these were representative of the population targeted. The
outcome could then be measured against the targets set. To gather information on who the respondents are, it is important to monitor by gender,

race and so on (see Chapter 6 for more information on performance indicators, monitoring and equalities).

Overpowering the public

Sometimes what was meant to be an empowering exercise becomes 'overpowering' for members of the public. It is easy to underestimate the effort it can take to get involved. People may 'pluck up courage to speak at a meeting and are then utterly deflated when they aren't called. If they are, they may be so nervous they can barely speak or they ramble on' (Beresford and Croft 1993: 52). People feel confused about procedures, feel they can't cope and are reduced to silence. It isn't easy to 'make the connection between our private troubles and public policy' (Beresford and Croft 1993: 130). To overcome these barriers organizers need to be aware of the way people might feel and offer training in what involvement may mean to them.

Public involvement is not easy; it brings many difficulties, not least conflict between communities and organizations. Conflict and how to avoid or minimize it is discussed in Chapter 8. With different needs being expressed by different groups of people, deciding on which decisions to adopt will largely be influenced by the organization's core values, aims and objectives. These are part of the organization's policy. In the next chapter I will tackle policy development and implementation for equalities.

5

DEVELOPING AND IMPLEMENTING EQUAL OPPORTUNITIES POLICIES IN SERVICE DELIVERY

Earlier chapters in this book argued for having equal opportunities policies (Chapters 1 and 3). This chapter will look at ways of developing equal opportunities policies in service delivery and ensuring that they are implemented. Certain aspects of a policy need to be in place for legal reasons and the legal aspects are non-negotiable. These should be made explicit in any policy. But to be effective a policy should go beyond legal requirements and, of course, must be implemented. A paper policy agreed by all but resulting in no change in services is of no practical use (although it may serve certain political ends).

A key part of a successful equal opportunities policy is the production and publication of a statement of intent (this should cover the organization's equalities aims and objectives). A policy based on the aims and objectives can then be drawn up. An action plan to implement the policy could then be developed. Outcomes should be monitored, progress evaluated and the action plan reviewed. All these stages are considered in this chapter. The chapter also looks at equalities policies on specific issues (on disability or harassment for example).

Mainstreaming equalities

An equal opportunities policy is more likely to be effective if it is part of a series of related measures such as equal opportunities policies on staff (Chapter 1 describes some of the links between equal opportunities in employment and in service delivery). Policies affecting staff are important since they will determine the culture within which equalities operates. Camden Council, for example, has linked employment and service delivery under the banner of 'Valuing Diversity'. This provides a stronger focus on the relationship between a diverse workforce and the council's ability to deliver services in diverse ways. Having a policy on equal opportunities in service delivery within a traditional white male culture is unlikely to be successful although it is better than having no policy at all. The aim of the organization should be to build an integrated equalities framework in which strategies relating to employment and services can support each other. Integration with initiatives overlapping with equal opportunities is also important, for example with policies on customer care, on quality work initiatives, on partnership initiatives with the community or on user involvement. The Local Government Management Board argues that any organization should be viewed as a 'system' where everything is interconnected. When systems are closed (work in isolation) they become irrelevant and cease to meet the needs of their customers. If systems are open they interrelate with other issues and are able to change to meet the needs of the community: 'this requires the effective management of the boundary between the "inside" and the "outside". Thus, the role and actions of managers is a key component in making the organisation effective' (1991: 34). The 'inside' could mean the whole organization or individual sections within it, 'outside' could mean the public or other sections within the organization. Some sections could be themselves very forward-looking and force the pace. They would be ahead of the game and force others to follow and to link in. So, individual sections could be crucial to any organization when they are leading the way and helping change. Stubbornly isolated sections, which drag their feet, are negative and unhelpful.

Equalities should be reflected in the 'core values' of an organization or its overall vision or mission statement, and linked to an overall strategic plan. UNISON, for example, has as its core values: 'Democracy, accountability, solidarity, cooperation, communication and education, equality, partnership'. From these values UNISON developed a series of aims which include one in which the Union would 'achieve equality of opportunity for all disadvantaged groups and individuals within UNISON and in the communities in which they live and work' (UNISON 1995: 21–2).

Equalities policies need to be endorsed by senior management with clear lines of responsibility and accountability for ensuring that the policy is implemented. Sylvia Pearce, whilst Chief Executive of Reading Council, commented: 'we are beginning to look at a different approach which involves ensuring that top management themselves personally emphasise their commitment to equalities . . . It's this stretching of the boundaries all the time, not from a "we know best" perspective but a "what is the next question we need to ask?" perspective' (LGIU 1995: 7).

If equalities is seen as marginal, policies will be ineffective. Sometimes attitudes towards equalities work are hostile or indifferent, and if allowed to persist these will hamper development. To be effective, all staff should embrace the equalities concept. Many on the shop floor see equalities as 'in the province of middle or senior managers, or personnel management functions, rather than affecting the day-to-day work experience of the individual's role in the organisation' (Blakemore and Drake 1996: 194). All staff need to own equalities issues. One way to achieve this is by publicity or training (see section on implementation below): 'Unless all employees can see the benefits of such strategies, and unless the majority are brought into the process of developing and implementing them, equalities policies are likely to be disowned and derailed. Sustained change towards greater equal opportunities and diversity, according to this view, is achieved through experimentation, learning from mistakes and a succession of limited changes' (Blakemore and Drake 1996: 213). More discussion on problems which may be encountered with resistance from staff can be found in Chapter 8.

The aim is to embed equalities into the work and culture of the organization. Implementing policies on equalities can also be built into the performance appraisal of managers: 'Equal opportunities must be an integral part of the management and organisational process. It is not something to be tagged on or seen as an optional extra. Equal opportunities is like holding up an X-ray to the organisation so that one can see it for what it really is' (LGMB 1991: 32). This requires leadership from senior management with a strong vision of where the organization sees itself on equalities issues. Several years ago, Haringey Council adopted this strategy under the banner of 'mainstreaming equalities': 'Mainstreaming is concerned with the further integration and development of the equalities dimension into all of a council's activities in the area of service delivery and employment. It is concerned with seeking to create cultural change in the organisation so that eventually an equalities ethos will pervade the work of all officers' (London Borough of Haringey 1991: 7). Haringey Council also believes that mainstreaming 'demands that equal opportunities becomes every officer's responsibility and in particular becomes an integral part of sound management' (London Borough of Haringey 1995b: 6). British Gas takes a similar view: 'How does an equal opportunities mission get translated into plans of actions? British Gas is doing it in the most powerful way possible – through line management commitment and involvement across the entire business . . . So all the business unit managing directors are holding planning workshops for their management teams . . . The workshops, which are facilitated by external consultants, have a very practical purpose and outcome' (*Gas News* 1994). The outcome of each workshop is an action plan with targets to be met.

In order to move the whole programme forward it helps to have a senior manager in overall charge and for there to be a structure in place leading on equalities work. Some central equalities function is advisable. Leaving equalities to managers in different sections without a centralized function could leave managers isolated. It could also mean that managers might be more loyal to their own section work than to any equalities work. This could lead to equalities being marginalized. As an extension of this, if equalities is solely a centralized function, with no devolving of responsibility to managers in sections, equalities could remain marginalized from the day-to-day work of the organization. Ideally there should be a central function for equalities work as well as responsibility placed on managers throughout the organization. The central function could be carried out by an equalities officer (reporting to the senior manager responsible overall), or a unit or a team of senior managers from across the organization meeting regularly and reporting to a central committee system. Gurbux Singh, Chief Executive of Haringey Council, argues that there is a 'need for a small centralised corporate equalities structure providing a developmental, research and monitoring function, primarily focused on service delivery . . . and mainstreaming planned over four or five years . . . with effective monitoring and evaluation, both to monitor initiatives and those responsible for their implementation' (LGIU 1991b: 6). The Local Government Management Board sees the centre's role as 'characterized as creating value for network partners, acting as leader, rule setter and capability builder, and simultaneously structuring and strategizing' (1996b: 26). Managers in senior positions could act as 'champions' for the programme. Each organization will have to develop structures suitable to its own internal arrangements. For organizations with elected members (e.g. local authorities), governors (colleges) or boards of directors there may be a need to have two structures – one for the most senior level of decision making and one for managers who advise the senior level and deliver the decisions. In local authorities, for example, it is common to have an Equal Opportunities Committee or subcommittee (of a policy committee) on which elected members sit, and a senior managers' group representing all council departments. Both of these structures would normally be serviced by a small central unit of specialist equalities officers. In addition, individual managers within different sections can be given responsibility for equalities within their section. This happens in British Gas where there are specialist staff to advise customers who are elderly or disabled: 'a team of customer service advisers . . . will have sole responsibility for home visits and related services . . . and will devote all their time to our older and disabled customers as we aim to improve our already high level of service' (*Gas Care News* 1995/1996). Specialist staff can also run specialist services for customers. British Gas, for example, runs a telephone helpline for non-English speaking customers with 140 languages on demand. The helpline deals with account enquiries, requests for supply, meter readings and energy efficiency (*Gas Care News* 1995/1996). At some point in the structure, trade unions need to be involved to ensure that all stakeholders in the equalities field own the issues.

Developing general equal opportunities policies

It is best to develop an equal opportunities policy that fits the organization and is written by those who work for the organization. Simply adopting some 'model' policy or taking from someone else's policy is unlikely to be as efficient as parts of it may not be relevant to the organization. Policy development can be done by setting up a small working group to undertake the work or by getting an outside consultant to develop the policy in a training session with a group of selected staff. Both methods work well. In either case it is important to consult widely on the policy with staff and trade unions. In developing a policy it is important to take account of where the organization is in terms of equalities and capacity for change. In developing specific policies on particular equalities issues (see section below for examples) it helps to involve service users.

There is no universal prescription as to what an equal opportunities policy should cover. What follows are basic elements which could be used in the development of a policy. The content of a policy should be determined by the needs of the organization, to satisfy what the organization is trying to achieve. The organization's goals could form part of the 'vision' or statement of intent.

This should answer the question, 'Why is the policy being formulated?' From this question the rest of the policy should flow. The policy should be like a 'manifesto' of what the organization will do and should include specific aims and objectives, key principles etc. At the same time it should be flexible enough to allow for necessary changes to occur: 'the core values thus become the markers around which discretion may be exercised' (LGMB 1991: 121). Working within the policy an organization should be able to make and maintain change. The policy itself should stand for several years, while specific action points drawn from the policy will change from year to year. These specific action points could be seen as a 'strategy' for action and form the implementation plan (more details on this in the last section of this chapter). The strategy would show how a policy would be made effective. This section looks at possible contents for an equal opportunities policy (service delivery) with some examples.

The statement of intent or 'vision' should outline the organization's philosophy. It represents the overall commitment which the organization has on equal opportunities. The Local Government Management Board argues: 'Developing a vision is a creative process, and therefore such techniques as brainstorming or visual representation are useful devices to employ' (LGMB 1991: 116). A vision can be derived from the 'core values' of the organization and could be as simple as: 'to ensure that each and every customer is served according to their needs'. The London Borough of Haringey's statement of intent has: 'In the provision of services and the employment of staff, Haringey council is committed to promoting equality of opportunity for everyone. Throughout its activities, the council will treat all people equally . . . It will not discriminate on the grounds of age, colour, disability, ethnic origin, gender, HIV status, marital status, nationality or national origins, race, religious beliefs, responsibility for dependents, sexuality or unrelated criminal convictions' (London Borough of Haringey 1995b: 6). The University of Central Lancashire states: 'The University will pursue not only the letter of the law but also the spirit of the law in relation to disability, race, colour, ethnic/national origin, sexuality, gender, marital status, age, or religion.' The statement includes reference to published material which 'will reflect this policy statement'; it includes a commitment to monitoring equalities in terms of staff and students and it covers 'persons not employed by the University but who are affected by the University's activities, such as visitors or contractors' (University of Central Lancashire 1993). Marks and Spencer's statement has as its final paragraph: 'The Company is responsive to the needs of its employees, customers and the community at large and we are an organisation which uses everyone's talents and abilities and where diversity is valued' (Marks and Spencer 1996: 15).

Overall aims and specific objectives can be derived from the statement of intent. Overall aims could be:

- Equal access to the service, for example no-one should be excluded because of disabling barriers to the building or because they speak a different language from the staff.
- Equal treatment within the service, for example Black people should

have the same opportunity as white people to occupy single rooms on a ward.
- Freedom from harassment, for example an effective procedure for dealing with harassment on grounds of gender, skin colour etc. from staff or other people using the service.
- Positive action to compensate for previous inequalities; for example, if few women use a day centre, taking action to make it more attractive to women and actively encouraging them to come.

(Read and Wallcraft 1995: 20)

To equal access and equal treatment, some organizations add equal share and equal outcomes. Equal share means 'a quantitative measure: the proportion of people using services reflects their particular needs and characteristics and the proportion employed in them reflects their skills and numbers' (Beresford and Croft 1993: 77). Equal outcomes focuses on results rather than intentions. Specific objectives within an equal opportunities policy could include this requirement: 'that services are based on consultation with those who receive the services . . . that services are flexible and responsive to the changing needs in our community, that information on services is widely available . . . that all council services will be systematically planned on an annual basis . . .' (London Borough of Haringey 1995b: 13). Haringey's policy also includes employment objectives, 'promoting equal opportunities through influence' and training objectives.

Policies should make clear who is responsible for the policy including its implementation. The University of Central Lancashire makes all employees and students responsible for their actions and all line managers responsible for delivering the policy.

Policies can also include sections on general principles for action or practice and procedures. Haringey Council's policy, for example, has a 'statement of principles for each equalities area'. These statements outline principles for people with disabilities, for lesbians and gay men, for black and ethnic minority communities, for women, for people with dependents, for people with HIV infection and for those experiencing age discrimination (see Chapter 2 for the kind of issues which could be outlined in such sections). Similarly the University of North London has in its Equal Opportunities policy principles for combating racism, sexism, prejudice against people with disabilities, heterosexism and prejudice against people with HIV/Aids. Some policies also include sections on good practices with regard to the use of language (for example the University of Central Lancashire).

A policy should contain a summary of the legal situation (see Chapter 3). It should have a section on monitoring policy implementation and on policy review. Some policies also have sections describing how to make a complaint and procedures to follow if policies are breached. Haringey Council's policy, for example, states: 'The Council will take disciplinary action within agreed procedures where the Policy is being abused, ignored or breached. It will be a condition of service that employees adhere to the Equal Opportunities policy and failure to do so will be cause for disciplinary measures to be taken' (London Borough of Haringey 1995b: 24).

Specific equal opportunities policies

In addition to general policies covering all aspects of equal opportunities in service delivery, many organizations have specific policies. Some are written as policies and some appear to be simply instructions to staff to do certain things (e.g. a supermarket which asks managers to provide trolleys for wheelchair users and trolleys with high shelves for people who cannot bend down). Although these are merely 'instructions' it would be fair to say that such organizations have 'unwritten policies' on disabled and elderly customers. An example of this is the services provided by British Gas for its disabled and older customers.

Some organizations have specific policies on particular target groups (e.g. women or disabled people). For example, English Heritage has a policy on disability in which the organization states that it 'seeks to ensure that its programmes and activities are accessible to everyone, wherever practicable. It aims to provide easy, dignified access to its own estate whenever this can be reasonably done, and encourages others who own or manage historic build-ings, or other heritage properties, to adopt access plans which are consistent with the special architectural, historic, or archaeological character of the property concerned' (1995a: 1). The policy document also contains guidance notes on conservation and access requirements aiming to 'promote simple, uncomplicated movement up to, into, and around historic properties' (1995a: 2). It points out that making a building accessible benefits everyone: 'The strategic approach advocated will also help to meet the requirements of people with sensory and other disabilities, of parents with small children, of older people, or of those suffering from temporary illness or injury.' The policy covers the Disability Discrimination Act and how to draw up an Action Plan. Examples of good practice are quoted. One refers to Winchester Cathedral which has a platform lift, a tactile model of the cathedral which is part of a 'Touch and Hearing' exhibition and a ramp made from paving stones. In their *Guide for Visitors with Disabilities* (also available in large print, tape or Braille), English Heritage states that its objective is 'to ensure that important landmarks are accessible to all' (English Heritage 1995b: 1). Within this, English Heritage specifies: 'For visitors with disabilities this does not just mean access in a physical sense, but also through the appeal to the senses of touch, smell and sound' (1995b: 1). The guide has sections on 'visitors with physical disabili-ties', 'visitors with visual or hearing impairments' and 'visitors with learning difficulties'. Another example is Westminster City Council which adopted a policy on disability with an action plan in 1997. The policy was developed following an audit of facilities and consultation with the community. This background work included qualitative research, running different focus groups for older people, voluntary sector providers, carers of disabled people and parents of disabled people. As a result of this work the policy developed covers information and communication, access to services and 'making the city of Westminster an accessible place to live, visit and work in' (1997). The Disabled Persons' Transport Advisory Committee (DPTAC) has produced a policy outlined in a leaflet for taxi drivers on *Meeting the Needs of Disabled Passengers* (1995). This includes vehicle design and maintenance, drivers' attitude and understanding, safe travelling positions and other good practice guidelines. Warner Brothers has an access policy which includes introducing wheelchair access and induction loops to all its cinemas.

The Football Association (FA) does not have a written policy on racism but there is clearly an unwritten policy that underpins its campaign, 'Kick out Racism' (see Chapter 1). The FA has as one of its aims 'to promote football as a participation and spectator sport which is open to everyone. Racism presents a major challenge to this aim. Anything which inhibits any group in society from watching or playing football has to be tackled by all who are interested in the future of the game' (CRE 1995c: 4). In its literature it states that the overall aim of the campaign 'is to ensure that people who play or watch football can do so without fear of racial abuse or harassment, whether verbal or physical' (CRE 1995c: 2). To this it adds more specific objectives: 'To encourage the right behaviour on the pitch through a code of conduct and fair play awards; to wipe out racism and intimidation among spectators; to persuade the government to amend the law on racist chanting or better enforce the present law; to introduce awards for anti-racism and anti-intimidation in football; to work with organisations at the grassroots of the game; to work with schools and local authorities to reach young people and win their support for the campaign' (CRE 1995c: 2). It also has an action plan (see below). Some councils have produced corporate policies on racial harassment to cover all services (housing, education, social services and so on). The London Borough of Hounslow has a corporate policy which includes a statement of intent, the legal background to the policy, a definition of racial harassment, procedures for dealing with cases (victims and perpetrators), inter-departmental and inter-agency work. There is also a section on policy implementation which includes training, publicity, monitoring and review (London Borough of Hounslow 1990). Housing associations have also adopted harassment policies. The London Housing Unit has produced a guide on sexual harassment for housing organizations (1991) covering staff and tenants and behaviour such as assault, false imprisonment, threatening telephone calls or letters, verbal abuse and rape.

Organizations can adopt specific policies on specific areas covering all target groups. For example, policies on harassment could cover more than just race. Such policies exist particularly for housing and cover harassment of one tenant by another. Sometimes they also cover harassment by staff of tenants or tenants of staff. Cardiff City Council has this written into its tenancy agreement which states that as a condition of tenancy 'you agree *not* to . . . do any acts which may cause nuisance or annoyance to persons living in or near the premises. This includes harassment because of someone's race, colour, religion, sex, sexuality, or disability which may interfere with the peace and comfort of, or cause offence to, any occupier, member of his or her household, visitors or neighbours' (City of Cardiff 1994). Some organizations have policies on consultation (to consult with the community using their services and how such consultation will be conducted). Other examples would be policies on specific services to specific communities. For example, Translation and Interpretation Units offer services to those who do not speak English and to deaf people. The Association of London Government published

Translators and Interpreters Services – A Handbook for Local Authorities (1997b) which covers policy and practice. The guide includes codes of practice for translators and for interpreters as well as standards of service.

Organizations can combine together to produce joint policies on specific areas of joint work. For example, much inter-agency work is done on domestic violence. This is largely an equal access issue. In Croydon a partnership of organizations from the public, private and voluntary sectors (Croydon Domestic Violence Joint Planning Team) produced a 'Protocol' on domestic violence (1997). The Protocol has a statement of intent which includes: 'Agencies who are signatories to this policy believe that domestic violence is a crime and that every woman has the right to live her life free from fear, intimidation and violence.' There is a definition of domestic violence: 'Domestic violence is an abuse of power where a known man uses physical, emotional, economic, sexual or psychological means to exercise control within the context of a close relationship between adults.' There are overall principles on issues of safety and confidentiality and good practice guidelines. Agencies signing up to the Protocol included the police, probation services, the local authority, the local health authorities, firms of solicitors and voluntary organizations such as women's refuges, rape crisis centre and so on.

Implementing policies

However well-meaning, policies that are not implemented serve little purpose. Once a policy has been formulated and adopted, it needs to become part of the working practice. A policy could start with a vision, from which aims and objectives are derived, but it must be implemented and in doing this the objectives need to be translated into a series of clearly defined tasks.

English Heritage says in its policy: 'The first step towards satisfying these aims is a comprehensive assessment of an historic property's access requirements resulting in an "Access Plan"' (1995a: 5). English Heritage specifies that the access plan should meet the needs of the property as well as the needs of users. Each plan must be specific to the building and must include priorities for action, management arrangements, timescales and periodic reviews. English Heritage also provides a checklist to help managers draw up the action plan which is in the form of questions to be answered on identifying access needs, considering ways in which these can be provided without alteration to the building and questions to ask if alterations are necessary (1995a: 7).

The Football Association has a ten-point Action Plan for football clubs to implement its objective to 'kick out racism'. The plan is as follows:

1 Issue a statement saying that the club will not tolerate racism, and will take specific action against supporters who engage in racist abuse, racist chanting or intimidation. The statement should be printed in all match programmes, and displayed permanently and prominently around the grounds.
2 Make public announcements condemning any racist chanting at

matches, and warning supporters that the club will not hesitate to take action.

3 Make it a condition for season ticket holders that they do not take part in racist abuse, racist chanting or any other offensive behaviour, such as throwing missiles onto the pitch.

4 Take action to prevent the sale or distribution of racist literature in and around the grounds on match days.

5 Take disciplinary action against players who make racially abusive remarks at players, officials and supporters before, during or after matches.

6 Contact other clubs to make sure they understand the problems and the club's policy, and have a common strategy for removing or dealing with supporters who are abusive and breaking the law on football offences. If it is dangerous or unwise to take action against offenders during the match, they should be identified and barred from all further matches.

7 Make sure that stewards and the police understand the problems and the club's policy.

8 Remove all racist graffiti from the grounds as a matter of urgency.

9 Adopt an equal opportunities policy in the areas of employment and service provision.

10 Work with all other groups and agencies – such as the police, the local authority, the FA, the supporters, schools, youth clubs, sponsors, local businesses, the local racial equality council and local voluntary organisations – to develop proactive programmes and projects to raise awareness of the campaign and eliminate racist abuse and discrimination.

(CRE 1995c: 3)

Tasks should have outcomes which are specific, measurable, achievable, realistic and timescaled ('SMART') (for more information on outcomes and performance indicators see Chapter 6). An action plan could also include the name of the person who has the overall responsibility for each task and what the resources will be (including staffing resources). When calculating costs it is important to take into account the cost of *not* taking any action. The CRE and the EOC in their publication *Further Education and Equality* recommend that 'an action or implementation plan covers: the role of senior management, responsibilities and resources, desired outcomes and targets, timetables and timescales, methods for measuring progress and methods of consultation with the community, students and staff' (CRE and EOC 1996: 11). This is echoed by the Employment Department Group's *Ten Point Plan for Employers*: 'An action plan gives you and your staff a clear set of actions to take. It allocates responsibilities so that people know what is expected of them, and sets specific objectives and targets. It sets deadlines for the completion of your objectives and targets and specifies how and by whom progress on each part of the action plan will be measured and assessed' (Employment Department Group 1995: Section 2). This continues by listing the benefits of action planning: 'A properly drawn action plan: focuses everybody's attention on the key tasks to be tackled; encourages co-operation in achieving agreed goals; enables equal opportunities to be tackled like any other management task.' Action plans should start from the organization's current position and move towards where it wants to be (the aims and objectives). The CRE and EOC's guide, *Higher Education and Equality* (CRE, EOC and CVCP 1997: 73), recommends asking the following questions when preparing action plans: 'Where are we now? Where are we going? What action is required? How shall we know when we've got there?' To find out what the current situation is it may be necessary to undertake an audit as Westminster City Council did before developing its policy and action plan on disability. Their survey showed that, for example, there was no central access point for information and that poor information prevented disabled people from taking up services. As a result, the Action Plan under the objective 'Improving access to information and communication', has as action points to 'Investigate a disability helpline based at one stop services at City Hall by March 1999' and to 'Produce a one stop information pack on all services for disabled people by March 1999', with responsibility allocated to the departments of Education and Leisure (Westminster City Council 1997: 6). Action plans can also include specific reviews of service provision. How this can be done is outlined in Chapter 7. Action plans (sometimes referred to as 'strategic plans') need to be flexible enough to accommodate change if this proves necessary as the organization develops.

A strategy to implement equal opportunities should be developed in consultation with staff and trade unions and when completed communicated to all staff, the public and other companies with whom the organization has dealings. Getting staff to embrace the policy may involve internal publicity, production of guidelines or information sheets and training in equal opportunities and service delivery. In general, training is more effective if it is part of a wider equal opportunities strategy. Training can include simply doing briefing sessions, giving information on new policies and practices and raising awareness (changing behaviour and attitudes) as well as specific training on specific services (e.g. racism in sport). The London Borough of Croydon had in its action plan a commitment to train 10 per cent of all staff each year in an area of equal opportunities (the choice was wide: training in new legislation e.g. the Disability Discrimination Act, equalities and contracts, consultation, monitoring, anti-racism, harassment procedures and so on). When the London Borough of Hounslow relaunched the equalities policy in 1995 it did so by a campaign of posters, leaflets (see Figure 2) and briefing sessions for all staff (excluding teachers). Posters carried the following messages: one spelt out the meaning of 'Equalities' (as in Figure 2), another had a heading 'Face Values' with photographs of different customers' faces (representing different races, ages, abilities, genders), with a caption saying 'These people have many different needs but they have two things in common. They are all your customers and they all need to receive the same quality service. Are you equal to the task?' A third poster was headed 'Different Needs, Equal Service' with a caption saying '8 out of 10 of your customers are from one or more of the groups listed here. Although they all have different needs they deserve the same quality service. Are you equal to the task?' The list along the side of the poster included older people, disabled people, women, lesbians, gay men,

E quality in service means:

Q uality public services

U nderstanding differences

A nswering to customers

L ooking for improvements

I nvestigating complaints

T aking time to listen

Y our responsibility

Are you equal to the task?

▓ Hounslow
Challenging disadvantage.

Figure 2   Spelling it out

ethnic minority people, black people. The posters were displayed in all work-places throughout the borough. For the briefing sessions a special video was produced to convey the council's policy in terms that all staff could under-stand and relate to. Fifty managers were then trained as facilitators and took it in turns to run two-hour briefing sessions with staff from across the council (mixing departments and grades). The aim was to train several thousand staff in 18 months. The *Spelling It Out* leaflets gave a definition of equalities work within the council: 'The Council's purpose is to serve the people of Hounslow and meet the needs of all its residents. There are, however, significant numbers of people in the Borough who, for one reason or another, do not receive all the services to which they are entitled. The idea of "Equalities" is simply about ensuring that everybody has the opportunity to take up services provided by the Council – by you, in fact.' The leaflet gave contact numbers for more information, outlined ten steps anyone could take to improve services from an equalities perspective, gave statistical information on customers and examples of good practice (London Borough of Hounslow 1995). The whole programme cost in the order of £20,000.

Other examples of specific guidance for staff include Marks and Spencer's booklet to staff, *Welcoming Disabled Customers*, published by the Employer's

Forum on Disability (1996). The guide includes statistical information on disabled people ('1 in 4 customers in the UK is either disabled or has a disabled person in their immediate circle'), and with clear pictorial illustrations emphasizes the importance of using appropriate language and offers tips on how to help customers with different forms of disability. Some information leaflets for staff can address specific questions front-line staff might be asked by the public. The Leisure Department in the London Borough of Hounslow produced a leaflet for its staff with answers to the questions staff are most commonly asked by customers. Examples of questions answered include, 'Why does the department provide women-only activities and events?' 'Why does· the department provide events for the lesbians and gay men in the community?' 'Why does the department provide specialist language material?' 'Why does the department provide multicultural events?' 'Why do you need this monitoring information on the Library application form?' (London Borough of Hounslow 1994b). The leaflet also gives contact numbers for staff to get help when asked questions they have difficulty in answering.

When dealing with outside agencies, an organization can have leaflets which outline its policy on equal opportunities. When dealing with customers, leaflets can outline the policy, raise awareness on specific issues or draw attention to particular services relevant to specific groups. All this information should be available in community languages where appropriate, in large print, on tape and in Braille. The London Borough of Croydon put up posters and distributed leaflets to its customers outlining its commitment to equalities (see Figure 3). The London Borough of Hounslow raised awareness on age discrimination by the display of posters and by giving away bookmarks with messages on them under the banner of 'Hounslow against Ageism'. For example, one had as its heading 'Age is Experience' and listed underneath: 'Leadership, Understanding, Resourcefulness, Knowledge, Inspiration, Support' as attributes of older people with messages on the back such as 'It is not how old you are but how you are old which matters' and 'Don't judge the person by their birth date'. The guide from English Heritage, quoted earlier in this chapter, is an example of information produced on services relevant to specific groups. The NHS 'Patient's Charter', which is an example of a public document with reference to equalities, is available in 11 languages other than English, in Braille, large print, sign language video and on audio cassette.

When producing documents of relevance to the public, mark the occasion by having a public 'launch'. It is important in changing services to celebrate success. When the London Borough of Croydon produced documents on consultation and monitoring which were part of its 'Plan of Action' to implement equalities, these were launched in 1997 under the banner of 'Equalities in Action'. Members of Croydon's diverse community were invited, along with staff working on equalities, councillors and the press. There was an exhibition on what 'Equalities in Action' meant in practice. Speakers at the launch included the Leader of the council, the Chief Executive, the chair of equalities, a service manager and an outside speaker who spoke about the importance of equalities from the community's point of view.

When equalities policies are implemented, services improve as they become more relevant to those who receive them. In the light of service changes,

Figure 3   Croydon's Equalities Commitment

policies can be evaluated and reviewed. Review dates and evaluation methods could be written into the policy or into the action plan. To ensure that services are changing and to evaluate them, outcomes of action plans need to be measured and monitored. This is the topic of the next chapter.

6

DEVELOPING PERFORMANCE INDICATORS AND MONITORING FOR EQUALITIES

The last chapter dealt with policy development and touched on policy implementation. To be able to ascertain if a policy is working and change is taking place it is important to evaluate progress. This can be done only if the targets have clear measurable outcomes. This is what performance indicators are for: they are a set of 'measures' which can be used to evaluate change. Performance indicators for equalities work are in their infancy but nevertheless the issue needs to be tackled. In order to set targets and decide on performance indicators the organization first needs to know base line data – where it is at present. For this it needs to 'count' or monitor who is receiving current services and assess what customers think of these services. The chapter looks first at monitoring, then at performance indicators and finally at benchmarking. Benchmarking or standard setting allows for comparisons between sections within an organization and from one year to the next as well as between organizations. A standard for service delivery which can be used for benchmarking in terms of race has been developed by the CRE. Other organizations have widened the CRE standard to include all equalities groups. Monitoring, performance indicators and benchmarking help to ensure efficiency and good management. To this end they are also required increasingly for financial reasons. Organizations which give grants or fund other organizations want evidence of success before money will be granted. The government requires local authorities to provide 'Best Value'. The aim of Best Value is to secure continuous improvements to service quality and efficiency. Best Value must start from the aims and objectives of the organization (as described in Chapter 5). Performance is then measured against objectives. There are also national standards and indicators set by the Audit Commission with which authorities can compare themselves. Local authorities are required to publish and report back on their performance against targets. Best Value is also looked at in this chapter. Much of the early part of this chapter is based on the London Borough of Croydon's publication, *Monitoring Equalities in Service Delivery* (1997d).

Monitoring for equalities

Monitoring for categories such as ethnicity and gender has been common for some time. In the late 1960s and early 1970s, schools began keeping statistics on 'immigrant' children. In the early 1980s, local authorities began monitoring their workforce and some service delivery (e.g. housing allocations). The government census monitored race for the first time in 1991; the criminal justice system started monitoring the ethnic origin of prisoners in the mid-1980s and of stop and search (whereby the police stop individuals on the street, on suspicion of intending to commit a crime, and search them for evidence) in the mid-1990s; more recently the health service started ethnic monitoring in 1995 (all monitoring dates quoted here are from CRE 1996c: 6–7) and the Crown Prosecution Service in 1996 (CRE 1996d: 7). Monitoring in terms of 'counting' who the service users are is much more difficult for service delivery than for employment. Indeed in employment it is relatively easy to count who the staff are and to draw up a profile of staff according to gender, ethnicity, disability and age. This is more difficult for services. It can be done where users can be counted, but for some services this is not easy or possible, especially those which are used by almost everyone (refuse collection, street lighting, water supply, inland revenue) – here measurement becomes more complex. In these cases counting the users will not help in determining who does not use the service as everyone does. On the whole, service delivery requires a more qualitative approach to measuring. For example, in the London Borough of Hammersmith and Fulham, all customers at sports centres were monitored in the mid-1980s and the result showed that there were equal numbers of men and women using the centres. However, detailed analysis showed that the use each group made of the centre was completely different; where men were taking part in sporting activities, women were accompanying children. This section will look at why monitoring is important, how monitoring should be done and which categories to choose for monitoring equalities.

Why monitor?

The aim of monitoring is to give a measure of the extent to which a service might be discriminatory. If an organization does not know who its customers are, it won't know whether women, black people, older people, lesbians and gay men or disabled people are using the service at all. Monitoring is therefore a crucial step in delivering services which cater for all groups of people. Monitoring allows the organization to tell if the service is discriminating against certain groups and whether people are getting what they want from the service. Monitoring therefore is a means of ensuring a high-quality service. By monitoring, for example, who the users of a sports centre are, it should be possible to see where the service is not meeting the needs of some groups of people and then improve the service accordingly. This is what happened in Hammersmith and Fulham sports centres. After initial monitoring, a survey was done looking at the reasons why women were not partaking in sport. This showed that women would take part in sport if they had childcare, women instructors, daytime sessions and well-lit premises. A programme of change was then introduced to meet these needs and subsequent monitoring showed an increased uptake of activities by women.

Monitoring also enables an organization to prioritize and plan services. It can reveal inefficiencies in the way services are run and help reallocate existing resources to target those most in need. A police division, for example, did not monitor domestic violence cases by gender. This meant that it was impossible to say how many of the victims were female or how many perpetrators were male. Even when figures were supplied there was no analysis of the particular situation in which male or female perpetrators were violent. An analysis over a period of time showed that when women were perpetrators, 'violence' was more often in self-defence and that when men were victims it was frequently from male partners. Until the male/female difference in domestic violence is clear, it will be impossible to provide appropriate police responses since without the recognition that it is predominantly women who experience domestic violence, responses are unlikely to be 'women friendly'. A similar situation occurs with crime generally. Police statistics rarely take into account the gender of offenders of crime. And yet Home Office statistics show that over 80 per cent of offences are committed by males. Until such figures are acknowledged, attempts to tackle the causes of crime by concentrating on 'young people' as opposed to 'young men' are bound to be less efficient.

Monitoring can show new opportunities for service delivery. It provides basic information to justify investment and allocation of resources into changing products or services. The marketing agency Saatchi and Saatchi regularly do research to find out what people eat, wear, like and think. However, this research does not monitor in equality terms those who are surveyed. It is therefore impossible to target products to certain groups of people. When Saatchi and Saatchi were asked why they did not monitor in this way their answer was, 'it just isn't something that gets asked . . . I suppose the researchers think people might find it embarrassing . . . and how many of these people are there anyway?' (Delin 1997). As we know from Chapter 1, ignoring the groups covered by 'equalities' can amount to ignoring the needs of up to 70 per cent of the population. Careful monitoring could gain access to a whole series of lost markets!

Finally, monitoring can demonstrate achievement. In the public sector and the voluntary sector, it can also help secure funding as most funding bodies now require evidence of customer numbers broken down by customer groups. For example, further and higher education funders require figures on student numbers broken down by race, gender and age.

How to monitor

To ensure the best result it is important to plan how the monitoring will take place well in advance. It is easier to build on what the organization already does. The method used for monitoring should be one that suits the service. If service users fill in application forms, questions monitoring race, gender, disability etc. can be added to them. These should be printed in the body of the form and not on a separate sheet. They should not be marginalized or kept secret. This means that overall outcomes of the monitoring should be collated separately and be reported but names and addresses not recorded for monitoring purposes; only collective data are needed. If most customers are met face-to-face then monitoring should occur at this point. Customers should not be monitored again and again unless it is part of a follow-up study to assess progress of a service. One example of bad practice given by the Centre for Research in Ethnic Relations concerns a borough where people presenting themselves as homeless were asked their ethnic origin on five separate occasions (Jones 1996: 40). This doesn't mean that monitoring should not occur at different stages, simply that customers should not normally have to be asked more than once. Monitoring could, for instance, then happen at the point at which a customer applies for a service, the point at which they are accepted for a service and the point at which they receive the services. For example, further education establishments are recommended to monitor applications, admissions, distribution by course, achievement levels and retention rates (CRE and EOC 1996: 12). On the whole it is best if customers are allowed to classify themselves, but this is not always possible. Decisions need to be made on how information will be stored (manually or on computer), who will have access to it and how it will be used. If it is not possible to monitor all customers (for example it would be extremely difficult to monitor all rail users), then regular 'snapshot' surveys could be carried out. Alternatively, information to test the relevance of the service to certain groups of people can be done in a qualitative fashion as opposed to quantitative 'counting' by using focus groups, or some other consultation methods (see Chapter 4).

For monitoring to be successful, someone needs to be in overall charge and staff need to know why they are undertaking the exercise, and feel confident in asking customers questions and in using the information. This may mean that staff will need to be trained. To reassure the public that the exercise is not meant to be intrusive, a form of words should be added to application forms or explained at the time of the interviews. The form of words suggested for use by staff in the London Borough of Croydon is: 'We want to make sure that we are providing this service fairly to everyone in Croydon, so it would really help if you would answer these questions about yourself. We want to use this information to improve our service to you, but we will ensure that all personal details will be kept confidential' (London Borough of Croydon 1997d: 5). Information collected can be compared with other organizations or with new information collected over a period of time to measure change. Data will only be meaningful if they are from a wide range of customers and not simply one group (in a supermarket, a 50 per cent response from those who shop in the evening is less meaningful than a 25 per cent response from customers throughout the day, unless you are interested in the night-time picture only). Data need to be properly analysed. One example of poor information comes from a crime survey undertaken in 1996 by one local authority. The survey was used to determine priorities in tackling crime on an inter-agency basis. The survey showed that racial harassment was not a top priority as only 15 per cent of residents surveyed had thought it important. What the survey did not do was to correlate people's answers with their ethnic origins. In fact monitoring by ethnicity had been done and 15 per cent of respondents were from a black or minority ethnic group. If these were the same 15 per cent who thought that racial harassment was a serious crime, then for them racial harassment might have been the most serious crime and should therefore have been on the overall list of priorities.

Categories to be monitored

Categories need to be agreed in advance and reflect the needs of the whole organization; they need to be consistent over time (or it will be impossible to measure progress); devised and collected in such a way that the data will be useful.

For ethnicity, it is sensible to use the government census categories. This means that there is a basis for comparison with the population at large or the local community. The census is carried out every ten years. Apart from the census other national data can be used as well as local surveys.

The census categories used in 1991 were:

Black Caribbean
Black African
Black other (please describe)
Indian
Pakistani
Bangladeshi
Chinese
Asian other (please describe)
White
Other

Some organizations add categories that are relevant to their locality. Since 1996, the London Borough of Croydon has added 'Irish'. In the 2001 census 'Irish' will be an official category. There are also pressures to add 'Black British' and a category for those of mixed parentage. The London Borough of Haringey has added categories such as 'East African Asian, Greek Cypriot and Turkish Cypriot'. It may also be useful to add a category such as 'Prefer not to answer', which may be more meaningful than a blank form which will not tell whether or not the questions were asked.

For gender, the categories are: male/female.

Age categories can be in multiples of five or ten, or they can describe a stage in life: pre-school, compulsory school, young adult, working age, retirement and so on. There will inevitably be some overlaps – for example the 16–29 age band includes both students and young people in work; here a combination of chronological age and life stage could be useful. The categories should be relevant to the nature of the services provided. In Croydon the categories chosen are:

0–4
5–15

16–29
30–44
45–59
60–74
75 and over

(London Borough of Croydon 1997d: 6–7)

For disability, it is best to ask: do you consider yourself disabled? Yes/No. If 'Yes', in what way?

Visually impaired
Hearing impaired
Mobility disabilities
Learning disabilities
Communication difficulties
Mental health problems
Other (please specify)

(London Borough of Croydon 1997d: 6–7)

Other categories which may need monitoring are sexuality, religion, language, dietary requirements or employment status. To monitor for sexuality it is important that privacy, anonymity and confidentiality are guaranteed or answers will be meaningless as customers will not give honest replies. For sexuality monitoring to succeed it is better to assess how accessible a service is to lesbians and gay men rather than attempt a 'head count' of lesbian and gay users. This can be done by using some of the consultation methods described in Chapter 4.

Some organizations find it useful to add an overall category of 'Not appropriate to ask' (for example at the time of an intervention by the police or social services) or 'Pending collection of data' or even 'Unable to classify'.

Setting targets

Monitoring for equalities needs to be in place before targets are set. Monitoring enables an organization to know who its users are. It also means that it is possible to measure progress. Monitoring can, for example, be used to see if the number of older customers increases over time. To ensure that change occurs many organizations set targets, which by definition are numerical goals. A target is different from a quota which is a number which must be achieved. So, for example, a sports centre may aim to increase its older customers by 10 per cent and introduce a series of measures to achieve this target. This would then be the goal to be achieved by a certain time. A quota would have meant that 10 per cent increase would have to be achieved; a target means that it is the figure which is aimed at but may not be achieved (see Chapter 3 for legality of using quotas). Targets should ideally be 'SMART' (specific, measurable, achievable, realistic and timescaled – see Chapter 5). They should be specific enough for anyone to understand what they are about; measurable so that change can be meaningfully assessed; achievable so that expectations are not raised too high; realistic so that they are effective in changing the organization (a target which over-simplifies reality or exaggerates a certain feature will be of little use even if it is easy to measure); and timescaled so that it is something which needs to be reached by a definite point in time.

Performance indicators

Targets are an indication of the future to be achieved. Performance indicators are about what has been achieved; they therefore measure the present. A target could be, for example, 'to increase usage by 10 per cent'; the indicator will be the number of people using the service. This can then be an indication of the extent to which the target is met. Indicators will allow an organization to measure progress against objectives set out in any action plan. Most organizations use performance indicators as a measure of success. Equalities indicators should be included in these. Indicators let the organization know whether equalities work is going to plan and how far the organization has got with its plan. For each objective of an organization (which will be translated into targets) there should be a performance indicator, so that people know when the objective can be said to have been met. A performance indicator should be a clear means of evaluating what has been achieved. For all indicators it is important that the reason for collecting the information is clear, as well as how information will be collected. Performance indicators should be such that they are agreed or acceptable to all those who are involved in the work as well as those measuring the work, and their interpretation should be consistent.

A performance indicator could measure outputs (a target could have been set for the number of older people attending a sports centre). Output indicators could include economy and cost (the target could be a percentage reduction in financial terms), efficiency and productivity targets (the target could be the percentage of occupancy or take-up), effectiveness (a target of reduction in complaints). Indicators could measure outcomes (the beneficial effects on older people from visiting the sports centre) or inputs (the amount of money or time spent to increase use by older people), and processes (the means by which older people were encouraged to take up sport – each of these could represent a task to be measured in itself). Output indicators are usually quantitative and measure achievement of an objective: the time it takes to respond to requests for service, completion times for certain tasks, the number of complaints received, the information put out (number of languages, amount available in large print or Braille). Outcome indicators also measure achievement but tend to be qualitative. They are on the whole more meaningful than outputs alone. How people see the service can be used as an outcome indicator, particularly if drawn from the results of surveys which are repeated in ways which allow change to be assessed. Input indicators give little information about achievement but do provide some form of measure and are a gauge of the organization's commitment. Process indicators can help to evaluate the effect of different strategies. They are largely quantitative but give a measure of the infrastructure in place to implement change. To this extent they also assist in mapping achievement. Once processes are well established and in place, they no longer need to figure as indicators. For example, developing systems to monitor uptake is an important indicator until monitoring is established. This could also be measured in stages: that a decision to develop monitoring systems is formally made, that preliminary research and work on the development is started, that the process is completed. Other process measures could be the production of documents (policies, guidelines).

At the very least equalities indicators should include:

- accessibility of the service: percentage of accessible building; accessible information (languages other than English, Braille); accessible staff (friendly, understanding issues of race, disability and so on); accessibility to the service by different groups (women may be targeted one year, disabled people the following year and so on)
- take-up of services: the number of customers from particular groups (this could be as part of an objective to match the percentages in the local community)
- outcomes: what percentage of disabled people, women, black and minority ethnic people and so on are satisfied with the service? Measuring the quality of service delivery is difficult; this can sometimes be translated into quantitative measures. For example, the quality of residential care could be in part measured by the number of single rooms, the number of social activities on offer and the number of times a resident can have a bath each week.

Examples of equalities performance indicators are found mainly in educational establishments and local authorities. The CRE and EOC suggest the following objectives for education:

- work placements are monitored for equal opportunities practice
- ethnic minority and women's organisations are consulted regularly
- the college projects itself in the community as an equal opportunity college . . .
- information and marketing material is provided in other languages, when needed . . .
- fair representation of ethnic minorities and women at all levels
- consistently high levels of student retention
- enhanced reputation in the local community
- increasing levels of customer satisfaction
- favourable publicity from the media
- wider range of employers offering work experience
- fewer grievances and complaints

(CRE and EOC 1996: 12)

The above objectives could be measured by the following indicators: the number of businesses led by women and people from ethnic minorities which provide work experience; awareness among outside 'stakeholders' of the college's equal opportunities policy; services catering for both sexes and all ethnic groups in the local community; college publicity and marketing

material which establish the college as an equality standard setter; targeting of
new students including both sexes and different ethnic groups (representative
of the community); effective equalities monitoring system; percentage of staff
who can demonstrate good understanding of equalities; percentage of students who can demonstrate good understanding of equalities; participation
rates for ethnic minorities and women in selected programme areas; drop-out
rates for all groups; levels of staff and student absenteeism including women
and people from ethnic minorities; number of grievances and complaints,
including those from women and people from minority ethnic groups (see
CRE and EOC 1996: 13). The manual continues by giving more specific
examples of measurements for each of these.

For local authorities, the Audit Commission (1997) sets the following
equalities indicators which have to be supplied on a yearly basis:

1 Number of the authority's buildings open to the public.
2 Does the authority have a published policy to provide services fairly to all
  sections of the community?
3 How does the council monitor its performance in implementing its policy?
4 Does the authority follow the Commission for Racial Equality and the Equal
  Opportunities Commission codes of practice?
5 Does the authority follow the Commission for Racial Equality's code of
  practice in rented housing?

These are, however, woefully inadequate as a real measure of whether services
are accessible and appropriate to the diverse needs of the community. The
Local Government Management Board, together with the Local Government
Associations, has developed indicators that give a better measure. For example,
under 'Information' the following indicators are suggested:

1   Information about services and customer satisfaction:
    1.1 Is it possible for people seeking information about or using council
        services at the main reception areas to do so by means of the
        methods listed below?
        (a) Audio tape recording and playback
        (b) Braille translation
        (c) Induction loop
        (d) Minicom systems
        (e) Translation of key documents into appropriate community
             languages
        (f) Community language interpreters
        (g) Sign language interpreters
        (h) Large print
        (i) Videos
    1.2 Indicate the percentage of main reception areas with each of these
        facilities (main reception areas are defined).
2   What percentage of council buildings (where there is access to a public
    reception area) have level or ramped access from the street or car park?
                              (Local Government Association 1997: 25–6)

Other indicators cover employment. There are also specific indicators for different services (housing, planning, leisure, education and social services). Housing, for example, has the following indicators:

1.1 The number of harassment incidents involving tenants, victims or complainants from the following groups:
   (a) Women
   (b) Black and other minority ethnic people
   (c) Disabled people
1.2 The percentage of racial harassment incidents resolved through the following:
   (a) Mediation
   (b) Legal action
   (c) Rehousing of the victim
   (d) CRE questionnaire procedures
   (e) Ombudsman
1.3 The percentage of racial harassment incidents unresolved.
2   The percentage of allocations to black and other minority ethnic households by different category of properties.
3.1 Do you have a procedure in place for recording incidents of sexual and/or domestic violence by tenants?
3.2 If yes, the number of incidents of sexual and/or domestic violence reported to a committee.
4.1 What is the percentage of households seeking acceptance as homeless in the following groups? Please specify by head of household.
   (a) Women
   (b) Black and other minority ethnic people
   (c) Disabled people
   (d) Lesbians and gay men
4.2 What is the percentage of households accepted as homeless in the following groups? Please specify by head of household.
   (a) Women
   (b) Black and other minority ethnic people
   (c) Disabled people
   (d) Lesbians and gay men
(Terms used are defined.)

(Local Government Association 1997: 27–9)

The government's drive for local authorities to achieve Best Value also requires the use of performance indicators. The principles of Best Value include the following:

- Achieving Best Value is not just about economy and efficiency, but also about effectiveness and the quality of local services – the setting of targets and performance against these should therefore underpin the new regime.
- Detailed local targets should have regard to any national targets, and to performance indicators and targets set by the Audit Commission in

order to support comparative competition between authorities and groups of authorities.
- Both national and local targets should be built on the performance information that is in any case needed by good managers.
- Auditors will report publicly on whether Best Value has been achieved, and should contribute constructively to plans for remedial action. This will include agreeing measurable targets for improvement and reporting on progress against an agreed plan.

(DETR 1997)

Equalities should also be an integral part of achieving Best Value.

Setting standards and benchmarking

In order to know how successful performance monitoring is, it is important to have standards by which comparisons can be made within one organization over the years or between different but similar organizations in any one year. Standards can be composed of a set of targets to be met. As with performance indicators, standards need to be accepted by those to whom they apply. Any organization wishing to attain a certain standard first needs to establish a baseline in order to be able to measure how far it needs to go. The CRE standard outlined below is one example which could be used by local authorities first to benchmark their race equality work and then to improve it. The CRE standard sets out to answer the following questions:

- What is the basic case for action on racial equality in local government?
- What should local government aim for in its work to develop racial equality action programmes?
- Which are the key measures that will translate policy and procedures into progress?
- How can progress be measured?

(CRE 1995e: 9)

All organizations benefit from benchmarking and setting standards: 'Benchmarking forces an external view against which to judge current objectives and standards; it requires the organization that is concerned with improvement to observe the best practices used outside their organization and creatively adapt them' (Clark 1992: 376). Large organizations with separate departments can benchmark internally. Standards can also be 'promises' to users of the service; these are found in the many 'charters' issued by different organizations. They represent a standard users can expect rather than a standard to aim at. This section is concerned only with standards to be aimed at and which can act as benchmarking for change.

The Local Government Management Board produced a set of benchmarking questions for organizations to see what they had achieved and what further action they need to take. This has been developed for local authorities but could be used for any organization. The answers to each question can be 'Yes', 'Partial' or 'No'. To achieve a high standard all answers should be 'Yes'; the aim is to reach that standard. Performance indicators will tell whether it has been achieved. Any answer will be a performance indicator. The questions are:

- Does your organisation have an equal opportunities policy?
- Does your organisation have a set of goals or targets on equalities?
- Does your organisation have a set of equal opportunities initiatives related to employment and personnel issues?
- Does your organisation have a set of equal opportunities initiatives covering service delivery?
- Do you have consultative meetings with specific groups – for example, older people, ethnic minority groups, women, the gay and lesbian community?
- Do you have staff whose job is to work specifically on equalities issues?
- Do managers behave in ways which model good equalities practice?
- Does the authority implement the CRE code of practice?
- Does your organisation have an access strategy for people with disabilities?

(LGMB 1991: 108)

The CRE, EOC and CVCP suggest that institutions ask themselves the following questions which can benchmark equal opportunities and higher education (these are a selection from their checklist). Again, although this applies to higher education, it could be adapted to be used by other types of organization:

Promotion of equal opportunities:
- How do the institution's mission statement, strategy plan and charter and public information material reflect its commitment to equal opportunities?

Priorities and action plan:
- Has the university developed an equal opportunities policy?
- Does the organisation spell out the implications of its equal opportunities policy for outside agencies, with which it does business? If so, how is this accomplished?

Ethos:
- Is there an agreed language policy and advice on the appropriate language to use in order to avoid discrimination or unnecessary offence?
- What steps are taken to ensure that important meetings are arranged at times which do not conflict with the family commitments of staff and students?

Awareness of the law:
- How is information conveyed to staff and students about the institution's equal opportunities policy, and their rights and responsibilities according to the law and the Charter for Higher Education?

Liaison:
- Are there established links with relevant, voluntary sector organisations catering for the needs of women, of various ethnic minorities or of disabled people?

Marketing of study programmes, research and other services:
- How effective is the marketing strategy in projecting the college or university as an equal opportunity institution?
- What information does the institution publish on the operation of its equal opportunities policy, including statistical breakdowns of student and employee groups by sex, disability and ethnic origin?
- Do the institution's publicity materials effectively reflect in visual images and language the existing and sought for diversity of the student and employee groups?

Monitoring, review and change:
- Does a senior manager have overall responsibility for the equal opportunities policy?
- How is the effectiveness of the equal opportunities policy monitored?
- How does the institution gauge whether staff and students are aware of the legal framework, student charters and associated equal opportunities policies of the college or university?

(CRE, EOC and CVCP 1997: 21–5)

A high standard would be achieved by answering 'Yes' to all these questions (specifying targets for those questions which do not require a 'Yes/No' answer).

The CRE standard for racial equality was developed for local authorities. It covers five areas with objectives to be measured and has five levels to be reached within each of these areas. Within each level there are several aspects of race equality to be met. The standard would then have to be evaluated through the use of indicators which would test performance to see if the standard is met. The areas described below are in themselves too vague to be measured.

The first area is 'Policy and Planning'. The aims are as follows:

- All employees, service users, contractors and organisations which come into contact with the local authority are aware of its racial equality action programme.
- The internal consultation process ensures that all employees are informed of the value of equal opportunity, and are committed to that policy.
- The local authority is able to evaluate progress towards achievement of its racial equality objectives.
- Members and officers have more comprehensive information from which to plan and implement the programme, internally and externally.

(CRE 1995e: 29)

Tasks under level one are on policies. Tasks under level two include the development of action plans, organizational structures and monitoring systems. Level three includes the development of targets and links with contractors. Level four includes equalities objectives in job descriptions and performance indicators for senior managers. Level five includes similar tasks relating to all staff and racial equality networks with other authorities.

The second area is 'Service Delivery and Customer Care'. What is being aimed at is that:

- The local authority's position on racial equality is clear to all service users and organisations with contracts, or seeking contracts.
- Staff in all service delivery directorates are clear on the policy and the action needed to implement it.
- The consultation process leads to greater satisfaction with the local authority's services from all sections of the community.
- Members of the public are aware that breach of the policy will be met with action from the authority.
- The local authority and its directorates are seen as standard setters on racial equality.

(CRE 1995e: 31)

Objectives under level one are on policy development for individual services. Under level two tasks include the establishment of ethnic monitoring, developing a consultative machinery to establish need and providing appropriate translation and interpreting services. Under level three tasks include ethnic monitoring becoming a standard procedure and monitoring the effectiveness of community consultation on influencing service delivery. Level four includes similar tasks to those for the 'Policy and Planning' area, but relevant to individual departments. Level five includes guidance to contractors and taking action against contractors who do not comply with racial equality commitments.

The third area is 'Community Development'. What is being measured is as follows:

- Community participation in the democratic process and structures of the local authority increases.
- The proportion of the population on the electoral register increases.
- There is greater involvement of the ethnic minority voluntary sector in the work of the authority.
- Take-up of council services widens across all sections of the community.
- The needs of ethnic minorities are systematically built into funding and development planning.

(CRE 1995e: 33)

Again there are a series of objectives outlined under the five levels of the standard. Area four concerns employment. It is in two parts; part one is on recruitment and selection and part two on developing and retaining staff. Area five is 'Marketing and Corporate Image'. What is being measured is as follows:

- All staff, and potential staff, are aware of the racial equality policy.
- Greater coverage of the local authority's policy in the media, including ethnic minority media.
- Greater involvement of all sections of the community in local authority public events.
- Community events are of direct relevance to a variety of ethnic groups.
- The authority is seen as a standard setter for racial equality.

(CRE 1995e: 39)

Other models of equality standards have been developed by local authorities to include all equality groups, not just race. These could be adapted for use by organizations other than local authorities. The following is an example developed by the London Borough of Hounslow and adopted with adaptations by Croydon. These standards are used as part of the service review mechanisms described in Chapter 7. There are standards for four general areas of service delivery work: meeting diverse needs, communication, user involvement and equalities environment. Within each area there are three levels to be met. For example, under 'Meeting Diverse Needs' there are two sub-areas, one on 'Understanding needs' and the other on 'Planning for quality and equality'. Each area has a list of performance indicators to measure achievement. The following is an example of performance indicators for the three levels to be met under the standard 'Understanding needs':

Level 1:
- Develop a profile of:
  (a) your current customers by target groups, and
  (b) the needs which your service meets
- Develop a profile of the wider population who would need to use your service.
- Identify any group(s) who are under-represented as users of your service and possible barriers to access.

Level 2:
- Undertake a 'needs' audit of users and potential users for your service to identify any gaps in service provision.
- Investigate in detail any one of the following barriers to accessing services and develop a service response:
  – eligibility criteria
  – physical access
  – customer support (e.g. interpretation)
  – cultural barriers
  – information on services
  – charging policy
  – perceptions of the service
  or undertake a follow-up survey of users who have withdrawn from the service to identify difficulties in the way the service is provided.

Level 3:
- Annual review of profile of service users to monitor the match with the population the service is designed to cover.
- Annual update of needs analysis to take account of demographic changes, customer comments, etc.
- Include an additional investigation of a specific barrier to access or the way service is provided in annual work programme and develop a service response.

(London Borough of Croydon 1997a)

Customers should have a bearing on what standards are set: 'Customers can directly influence standards through an ever more demanding specification and by complaints or suggestions made directly to the organization. They can also influence them indirectly by withdrawing their custom, telling the competition and regulatory bodies'(Clark 1992: 376). As mentioned in Chapter 4, service users can be directly involved in setting performance indicators and standards. Given that performance indicators are often about their needs and preferences, this approach makes sense. However, this must be done with care: 'if people are to take part in quality setting, they need to be supported with the information, confidence and skills to do so. This provides a basis for the joint monitoring and evaluation of initiatives' (Beresford and Croft 1993: 194–5). Without this approach there is a danger of being paternalistic. Ways of involving the public in reviewing services is part of the next chapter.

7

REVIEWING AND
CHANGING SERVICES

One of the most powerful means of changing an organization is to undertake fundamental reviews of the services it provides. This involves looking at services in detail and questioning whether they are appropriate to people's needs, then deciding how they should change, and finally, if necessary, changing them. In the public sector, service reviews are now required by the government as part of Best Value. In discussing service reviews, topics from the previous chapters are used. This chapter first describes the work done on 'quality' and service improvement including the links with equalities, then looks at equalities auditing and service planning, and finally at equalities service reviews. Much of this chapter is based on the STEPS model (Strategic Equalities Plans in Services) which is a process designed to review services, developed by the author for the London Borough of Hounslow.

Quality and service improvement

A system for continuously improving quality has been an aim of many organizations for some time. Approaches have varied and have included 'quality control', 'quality assurance' and 'total quality management'. In 'quality control', services are monitored to ensure that agreed standards are being met – for example, that there are clear standards which should be met for toys or food hygiene. In 'quality assurance', management systems are developed to ensure that good quality services are delivered. This would mean, for example, looking at the policy and procedures that are in place. 'Total quality management' involves a series of measures such as making a commitment to continual service improvement, changing the culture and emphasizing everyone's contribution to effective performance. Total quality management includes both quality control and quality assurance systems. As part of this process some organizations run 'quality circles' where groups of workers come together to discuss how to improve the services they run. A quality service can be defined as one that matches the 'visions' or aims and objectives of the organization and meets the needs of users in a way which is efficient, effective, economical and equitable. Quality of services can be improved by staff, involving service users and, through changing organizational systems, the organization's method of operation. For staff, working through the process will increase their own ability to meet user needs.

A quality audit can be undertaken to meet a whole raft of objectives. It can, for example, see if a service satisfies the needs of current or potential customers; compare levels of satisfaction with elsewhere; look at the environmental impact of the service; identify the costs involved in providing the service or see how efficiently and effectively the service is provided and whether it is making the best use of resources: 'quality audits look at the whole service and its relationship with customers. They are very different from the narrow accountancy-based value for money studies conducted by district auditors. To be successful they cannot just be an internal management study. They need to include the views of users and employees' (LGIU 1991a: 6). The following process is one that is often used in quality audits:

- First identify who your actual and potential customers are.
- Check why they are not using your service.
- What is your image?
- What is your product?
- How might they need to change?

(Beresford and Croft 1993: 179)

The maintenance of quality therefore involves planning and reviewing in cooperation with staff and users. Some people use a 'service cycle' in which planning is followed by specifications for change, specifications are then followed by implementation, and monitoring and review then follow implementation. The cycle then starts again with the planning stage.

Depending on the priorities attached to management decisions or user input, approaches to review may be 'top-down', where quality is driven from the top and decisions are handed down to front-line staff, or 'bottom-up', where quality initiatives are driven by front-line staff and informed by the views of users. There are advantages and disadvantages to both approaches. The advantage of a 'top-down' approach will be that it is led by those in charge, that is to say those with most power, and it therefore has an increased chance of being implemented. Moreover, such an approach is more likely to be accepted by managers and more likely to attract resources. However, the 'top-down' approach tends to be one removed from reality and may not have the impact on service changes that was intended. The 'bottom-up' approach is closer to the day-to-day delivery of a service. As such it is probably more likely to identify the problems correctly as those involved are more in touch with users' views and needs. On the other hand the approach is less likely to be able to influence those at the top of the organization of the importance of the project, the need for resources or the need for change. Both approaches have their value and examples of both are given in this chapter. The method chosen will depend on the service to be reviewed and the type of organization in which the review is taking place. The ideal may be a combination of both approaches.

The government's drive for Best Value is a drive for quality. It aims to improve poor performance within public organizations (see principles of Best Value outlined in Chapter 6). Where there is 'a clear prima facie case that an authority is performing poorly, it should initiate an urgent and fundamental review of the service and its performance: this will embrace both service objectives, the standards to which the authority aspires, and the means by which the service is delivered. It will seek to answer three key questions: what is expected? what is delivered? and how can things improve?' (DETR 1997). Under the Best Value scheme a local authority should review the poorest performing service areas first, and all service areas should be reviewed in a four- or five-year period. Reviews aim to improve performance, efficiency and quality management. Reviews should lead to an action plan with clear targets to be achieved. Part of Best Value also involves benchmarking against the performance of other service providers and other local authorities.

Auditing and service planning in equalities

An audit of the way service provision operates to meet the needs of users is often the first step towards changing a service. An audit can be followed by an action plan for change. Haringey Council has a well-developed means of auditing services from an equalities perspective. Each directorate is expected to carry out an audit of at least two areas of their activities each year and aim to complete auditing all their services within four years. Their audit, which follows a 'top-down' approach, could easily be adapted to fit other types of organization. The scheme used in Haringey is done by:

- identifying existing systems, procedures and practices that are in line with agreed policy;
- examining how well these meet the Council's equalities objectives;
- recommending remedial action where appropriate.

(London Borough of Haringey 1995a: v)

The audit is conducted in four stages: a questionnaire is distributed to managers; there is a follow-up visit to managers to clarify answers to the questionnaire; interviews are undertaken with relevant officers to check the answers; a report is written and sent to the service director and the Chief Executive.

The process starts with a service director identifying a service to be audited. A service manager completes and returns the audit questionnaires to an auditor. The auditor visits the service department to verify responses to the questionnaire. The auditor then writes a report which is presented to the service manager for comments. On the basis of the audit an action plan is drawn up. The agreed action plan is then incorporated into a service plan for the following year. Haringey awards 'Equalities Charter Marks' when remedial action has been fully implemented. The Chief Executive's role is crucial: he has to agree with each director which service is to be audited, receive the final report, agree on remedial action and award the Equalities Charter Mark. The service directors' role is also very important: they identify the service to be audited, remove any obstacles to the audit being carried out and ensure the implementation of the action plan. Staff from the organization are appointed as 'auditors'. Their job is to undertake the audit. Within this they need to collect evidence as proof of what the service providers are saying and look at how the service is delivered to ensure that actual practice is in line with policy and procedures. The auditors must also talk to front-line staff to ensure that policies and procedures are being followed in their day-to-day work. The questionnaire they distribute relates to the Council's 'Strategic Equalities Objectives'. For example, one strategic objective in Haringey is 'To base council services on the needs expressed throughout the different communities of Haringey'. The questionnaire for this objective is:

1 Do you have a mechanism for consulting your clients?
2 Does the mechanism take into account all of Haringey's communities? Does it use the Council's equalities categories?
3 Do you make special provisions for:
   (a) People who have difficulties with the English language?
   (b) People with disabilities?
   (c) People who need to make arrangements for childcare?
   (d) Lesbians or gay men?
4 Do you have a system to monitor the people who take part in consultation?
5 Does the system cover all the equalities categories?
6 Where certain groups are consistently under-represented at consultations, do you do anything about it?
7 Do you have a system for feeding views and data from consultation into the service planning process?

(London Borough of Haringey 1995a: 9)

Other strategic equalities objectives in Haringey include an assessment of the take-up of services by all sections of the community, provision of services that meet the needs of the community and identifying any imbalance (after monitoring). There are questionnaires relating to all these objectives too. A further objective is 'To promote equal opportunities through influence, ensuring that services which contractors provide for the Council meet the needs of all sections of the community'. The questionnaire to test the extent to which this objective is met includes questions on the tendering process. Questions relate to measures taken by the service section to ensure equalities in services put out to tender. They include questions on corrective measures which would be taken if contractors do not meet the council's requirements on equalities (more information on contracted services and equalities is provided in Chapter 8). The equalities objectives and associated questionnaires in this particular example also cover employment issues and training.

Service planning involves developing a systematic means of prioritizing work in order to achieve change. In addition to being important for efficiency and economy, service planning also enables an organization to target its resources where they are needed. It is usual to draw up a service plan on a yearly basis. It derives from the aims and objectives of the organization. In developing the plan different objectives are selected with the tasks needed to achieve them. This is a similar process to 'action planning' (described in Chapter 5), the main difference being that whereas service planning is usually a yearly task, action plans can run over a number of years.

An example of planning change in equalities on a yearly basis and which incorporates a 'bottom-up' approach was developed by the Social Services Department in the London Borough of Hounslow. Here each service manager (service managers cover a much smaller service area than that covered by directorates as in Haringey's auditing system) prepares an Equalities Management Plan. The plan takes into account the department's objectives, the needs of users and the resources available, and it also looks at constraints and opportunities. In this scheme each year the plan must identify one item from the directorate's equalities programme to work on. The service manager, together with a team of staff from the service, needs to develop a set of projects which will address the items identified and which are designed to make progress on equalities. The overall aim is to get teams to prepare and own their plan, develop knowledge on equalities and skills to undertake equalities work within the teams themselves. The equalities programme includes the following areas of work, from which a service manager can chose any one item for development of equalities work: Equal Opportunities Policy Statement; providing appropriate services; providing staff with relevant expertise and knowledge; consultation; record keeping and monitoring; communicating council services; policy on challenging racist/sexist/homophobic/disablist attitudes, stereotypes and expectations; supporting minority users; purchasing services; protection of customers; complaints; customer care; drawing up minimum service equality targets. At the end of the year the progress is evaluated and a new plan is drawn up with a new focus for work for the following year.

Equalities service reviews

Undertaking service reviews can form part of an overall action plan for changing the organization. In the London Borough of Croydon, every department prepares an action plan on equalities in service delivery each year. The plan may include a series of different measures (e.g. improving monitoring procedures, celebrating multicultural festivals). Action plans only include work which is innovative and will change the way the service is run. There is a real danger of managers including all work from their service area which relates to equalities rather than innovative work. Organizations may be tempted to produce such action plans, but while they appear impressive because of their great length, in reality they produce no change. They fail because they include much of the day-to-day delivery of services. An action plan is about change.

In Croydon action plans must also include which specific areas of service delivery are going to be reviewed in that year. Each department is expected to review one or two services a year. A service review involves the equivalent of taking the service apart, examining it and putting it together again in such a way as to improve it. The aim of a service review is to change service provision and to ensure that it matches the profile and needs of users and potential users. The planned outcome of a service review should be a specific action plan for that service indicating how improvements in service delivery will be achieved. This means looking at the current situation in terms of how the service is *delivered*, so asking such questions as: are there any duplications or gaps in service? How is the service managed? What are the resources? Who gets access to the service? It will also mean assessing whether the service is *effective*, including cost-effective? Are there unmet needs? Are people missing out on the service and if so why (what barriers are in the way)? Such a review will require inspection of what happens elsewhere and comparing practices to see where change could be made. Finally the review involves developing a plan for future action. The advice given by the Commission for Racial Equality, the Equal Opportunities Commission and Committee of Vice-Chancellors and Principals on service reviews is that managers should ask the following questions:

'Where are we now?' asks the user to list, where appropriate, what stage the institution or department is at. This may require a form of audit of present policy, provision, and practices and to assess the structures and procedures in place to carry out an audit. It may also involve liaison with other departments and senior management.

'Where are we going?' asks the user to list areas of priority, to establish overall aims and to set targets.

'What action is required?' enables the targets and action plan to be considered, tasks allocated and implemented.

'How shall we know when we've got there?' anticipates the monitoring and evaluation of changes. When the point is reached, perhaps on an annual basis, the user returns to the beginning of the cycle to consider a further audit/review of current position.

(CRE, EOC and CVCP 1997: 73)

An example of service reviews in equalities is those undertaken by the University of East London. In 1996, the University had asked, as part of its action plan on equal opportunities, that reviews looking to improve access for students with disabilities should be carried out by all departments during the following 12 months. In this instance the reviews included the following checks:

1 Daily contact with individual students is fully documented.
2 Enquiries from potential students and services outside the university which may advise potential applicants are recorded.
3 Two feedback questionnaires are sent out each year to (a) all students indicating a disability at point of enrolment and (b) all students in direct contact with services.
4 In-depth interviews with seven students with quite extensive impairments were carried out by the co-ordinator in July 1996 with the aim of securing feedback on the students' expectations and experiences at the

university to enable us to identify improvements needed in the university provision.

(CRE, EOC and CVCP 1997: 58)

Another system, developed by the author for Hounslow, is the STEPS (Strategic Equalities Plans in Services) model for service reviews. This is tailored for use by local authorities but could be adapted for other organizations.

In Hounslow, as in any other council, services have evolved over many years to meet a variety of needs. These include the needs of local residents, the needs of the council and the needs of central government. However, once council services are established the needs of residents often get forgotten. One problem is that the profile of the borough will change over time in terms of age, ethnicity and disability. A second problem is that the council tends to concentrate on its own needs, responding to financial and other problems, and this replaces the needs of the citizens it serves. If this occurs, the council may lose touch with its purpose of providing services to local residents. The aim of the STEPS model is to redress the balance by refocusing services on the community. The model takes a 'bottom-up' approach in which the review is led by front-line staff and involves users and non-users alike. The advantage of involving front-line staff is that this allows for their expertise in the day-to-day running of the service to be used. It also means that there is an increased chance that local residents are involved (many front-line staff live locally) and there is a greater chance that members of target equalities groups will be involved (there are more women, black and minority people at that level). In addition, involving front-line staff gives them the opportunity to be involved in work they would never normally be asked to do, and also provides a way of training them in equalities. Finally, any recommendations agreed as a result of the review are more likely to be implemented as staff who know what the decisions are about are more likely to own the recommendations, having been part of the team which drew them up. In my experience industrial relations problems which sometimes follow change in service provision (particularly if it involves a change in job descriptions) are less likely to occur if front-line staff are part of the process.

Senior managers do not need to be part of a review team but do need to be kept informed about the team's work. Clearly it is important that the team works on recommendations which are likely to be acceptable to the organization, and senior managers would have a feel for such issues. Problems could occur for instance where a recommendation did not fit the overall priorities of the organization or could not be met on financial grounds. Service reviews do not imply that further money needs to be spent on the service; indeed, there is a hope that the service will be changed but remain within existing resources. This may mean that some existing customers will lose services. However, the aim will be to make the overall service provision fairer to all members of the community. A service review of this type takes at least six months to complete. The steps to be taken in order to carry out a STEPS review are reproduced as follows.

1 *Choosing a service to review.* Questions which need to be considered include the following. Is the service well defined such that it is possible to

distinguish between what is part of the service and what is not? If the service is tendered out should negotiations be with the client or the contractor? Is the service of a size that is neither too large nor too small for a review? Reviewing the whole of a library service may be too big a task, but reviewing one service (book lending) within a branch may be too small (unless there were very complex issues to be addressed). Reviewing all the services a branch library provides or reviewing the whole of the book lending service or information service across all local libraries might be about right (see below for an example of a service review in a small branch library).

2 *Building up a team to undertake the review*. Each team should include front-line staff. Staff will need time off from normal duties and this will need to be negotiated with managers beforehand. Staff may need extra payment if meetings are out of their normal working hours. This too would have to be agreed before the review starts. The review team should also include the immediate manager of the service and staff from the department who have knowledge or experience of equal opportunities in service delivery. Where possible each team should include representatives of the target groups and ideally half the team should be women. The teams should also include representatives from minority ethnic groups. Disabled staff, older staff and lesbians and gay men should be included if at all possible.

3 *Defining the service*. The team should start by defining the service as they see it at present. This can be done through a brainstorming session. It should cover how the service is delivered, which particular groups are targeted and what help is actually given to those target groups in respect of access to the service. Views on what the service is trying to achieve may be different depending on the member of the team (manager, front-line staff). Defining exactly what the service is about is important because a review will be more successful if it starts from the 'reality' of the service.

4 *Equalities issues in the service*. The team should spend some time reviewing the equalities implications of their service. A review of the following questions is often useful:
- Who uses the service (this requires monitoring of users and analysis of the results)?
- Why do some groups not use the service (this requires consultation with the community)?
- Which groups should benefit most from the service?
- How do people comment or complain about the service (and how accessible is the complaints system)?
- How does the service respond to comments and complaints?
- How is information about the service disseminated? Is this accessible to people who do not speak English and to disabled people?
- How does the service evaluate whether information reaches, and is understood by, different groups of people?
- Are there performance indicators on equalities? How are these evaluated and used?
- How accessible is the service for women, black and minority ethnic people, disabled people, older people, lesbians and gay men?

5 *Drawing up an action plan for the review*. Once the equalities issues have been defined it is possible to draw up an action plan. The work which will need to be done includes monitoring and consultation of users and non-users. There should also be consultation with other front-line staff members. The team, which needs to have an overall timetable of action, will need to consider who is going to be responsible for each task, how often the team should meet to review progress and how information about progress will be fed back to managers.

6 *Working on the action plan*. This stage could involve using much of the information already available in the department. Members of the team should certainly look at consultation exercises done in the past, complaints received, customer records, client files, service reports, the results of questionnaires and population statistics.

7 *Analysis of all data received*. This may need expert help; in some instances analysis will require the use of a computer.

8 *Recommendations*. On the basis of the findings recommendations should be drawn up coupled with clear performance indicators. Any recommendation must take into account equalities issues, managerial issues and financial constraints. If the team is open to change, restricting proposals to fit existing resources should not necessarily inhibit action being taken.

9 *Negotiation*. Once agreed by the team, recommendations may need to be negotiated with senior management and with elected members. For a service with a contractor/client split it may be necessary to involve both sides in any negotiations.

10 *Implementation*. All service reviews will need to be reported to the corporate equalities group and to the equalities committee. Some might need to be agreed by other committees and this should have been established at the outset. Implementation should include feedback to staff and to the community on the outcome of the review.

11 *Evaluation and review*. After the recommendations from the review have been accepted, implementation must be monitored. Monitoring should be carried out at predetermined intervals such as every six months.

Example of an equalities service review

The following is an example of a service review in which the author was involved, using the STEPS model to review the work of a small branch library. The review team consisted of two members of staff from the library (the manager and one other), the departmental community librarian for ethnic minorities, a manager from the central library service, an Equalities Unit adviser and a community development worker for the local area. Of the team of six, five were women and two were Asian. The team first defined the services offered by the library. This revealed that the services were different from those assumed by both managers and by the library staff themselves. Neither had realized the extent to which they performed duties which were in addition to those specified in their job descriptions. Few books were actually issued by the library and the staff spent much of their time giving advice and helping people to fill in forms, commonly for housing benefit and other similar services. Library users were asked to fill in monitoring forms when they applied for library tickets but these forms were thrown away by the staff and so the information was not entered anywhere.

The team identified problems experienced by the library. There was a secondary school nearby but the library had no formal links with the school and few children from the school visited the library. A group of elderly Asian men came into the library every day and sat reading the papers but no one had ever spoken to them about their requirements. Several foul-mouthed girls, 11 and 12 years old, came in causing havoc on a regular basis. The girls would swear, knock the books off the shelves and generally make life difficult for all. Again no one had spoken to them about their needs but on occasions the police had been called to throw them out. Often, at lunchtime, people working in local businesses came in to the library; again no one had asked them what their needs were. There was a room in the library available for use by a health visitor who held classes once a week with young mothers and also by the local education department for classes in English as a second language. This room was underused and could be developed for other activities. The team drew up an action plan with timescales and allocated tasks to each other. The action plan included:

- Doing a survey of the local businesses to see what use they wanted to make of the library. This was done at a lunchtime open day.
- Asking the Asian men what they would like of the library service.
- Having a meeting with the girls to find out if they wanted to use the spare room as a meeting place.
- Contacting the GP's surgery next door, where various groups of older residents met with health visitors, to see if the older people would participate in a discussion group on the use of the library by older people.
- Monitoring customers and comparing the results with the make-up of the local population.
- Visiting the secondary school and inviting staff from the school into the library.
- Having an open evening with staff from the leisure department and inviting all the residents from local streets to attend.
- Doing a survey of the neighbouring streets to see who did or did not use the library and the reasons for their responses. Specialists in the council advised the team on survey techniques.

The review found that the Asian men wanted to be able to meet and play draughts; the girls wanted to be able to meet boys; most local residents wanted a point where they could get information on council services and access to complaints (broken pavements and so on); and the secondary school would welcome having a 'homework corner'. It would appear that local residents wished the library would become more like a community centre and less like a traditional library. Moreover, the local businesses were keen to sponsor some changes. The recommendations were then negotiated with senior managers and finally went to the Leisure Committee, following which implementation started.

There are sources of information to help with many of the types of work undertaken to change services which are described in this chapter. These include the Commission for Racial Equality, the Equal Opportunities Commission and the National Disability Council who will all give advice and can provide written information. The Local Government Information Unit and the Local Government Management Board both produce publications on equalities and related issues. This information could be used by organizations other than local authorities. Stonewall is a campaigning organization for lesbian and gay rights and produces information on that issue; it also gives advice over the phone. There are national disability groups (different organizations exist for different forms of disability e.g. Scope for people with cerebral palsy) which produce information and can offer advice on disability issues. There are organizations for older people who do a similar task (e.g. Age Concern). There are also journals which either specialize in specific equalities areas (e.g. *Disability Now*) or deal with equalities in general (e.g. *Equal Opportunities Review*). These can be found in major libraries.

Auditing and reviewing services is time consuming but without doubt is the most effective way of changing organizations and ensuring that services meet the needs of a varied public. Even if one uses all the information available and goes through some of the processes described above there can still be numerous problems to be solved. In all equalities work one encounters barriers which can frustrate the best efforts. These need to be overcome. Resolving problems and overcoming barriers is the topic of the next chapter.

8

BARRIERS TO ACHIEVING
EQUALITIES IN SERVICE DELIVERY

This chapter looks at some of the more common difficulties which may be encountered in implementing equalities in service delivery. It will review both problems arising with equal opportunities policies established and used within an organization and those that are part of a service that has been contracted out. The chapter also considers organizational issues that can act as barriers together with some of the problems managers face in introducing change. Finally, the chapter examines the specific problems which result from involving the public in the design of services. Problems and barriers are often ignored partly because equalities is still a young field and partly because people tend to write about success rather than failure. There are, therefore, few documented cases of failure and accordingly many of the examples given are known to the author personally or have been learned of through discussion with colleagues.

Equalities in contracted-out service

Every organization should ensure that its equalities policies are maintained in services contracted out to other providers. Normally this means organizations that have tendered out their services but it also includes organizations where there is a purchaser/provider split. That is to say, where services are bought from providers as happens in the National Health Service where GP fund-holder practices will buy the services of a hospital.

Increasingly services are contracted out in what has become a quasi-market where managers of the organization become purchasers of services. Where organizations were traditionally characterized by hierarchical cultures in which decisions were made at the top and instructions were passed down to those who delivered the service, now they are becoming characterized by a contract culture where decisions are made by the organization and handed to other organizations for delivery. However, in both arrangements managers are equally distant from users of the service. The manager's role remains one of policy making, while the implementation of policy is done by the contractor or service provider. Accountability becomes more complex. Thus, the provider can be held to account for failure to deliver a service to specifications but cannot be held to account for poor specifications. Equalities considerations in contracted services therefore need to be incorporated into the policies of the organization and into the specifications going out to tender.

With contracted services the same issues apply as with services run in house. Equalities policies and service standards should be determined in advance and included in all specifications. In this way specific requirements in terms of equalities can be included in the tendering documents. A specification can include, for example, a requirement that a sports centre should run so many sessions for disabled people, that it should provide a crèche, that it should advertise its services in different languages. The organization to whom the service is contracted can be asked to monitor its users to ensure that different target groups have access to the service and can be asked to consult with users and non-users. As part of the tendering process, specifications for the service being put out to tender can include a requirement to monitor and to consult. Specifications can also include details of the monitoring that should be done. The same applies to methods of consultation. Alternatively, organizations which tender for the work can be asked, as part of the tendering process, to specify how they intend to meet the needs of different groups of customers, monitor customers and consult users and non-users. These can all be part of the criteria established to select tenderers. How well contractors perform can also be measured against any stated criteria on equalities standards. Contractors can be monitored for service design, take-up of services, accessibility, attitudes of staff and training, policies and procedures and consultation with users and non-users. In their advice to those involved in higher education, the CRE and EOC recommend: 'In choosing between contractors offering services, colleges and universities will need to balance carefully their equal opportunities requirements with other quality factors and price' (CRE, EOC and CVCP 1997: 14).

Local authorities can specify equalities issues in the way services are delivered when contracting out services. This contrasts with equalities in employment where, in 1998, only race issues can be specified. This may be broadened by 1999 to other equalities groups. For example, the London Borough of Haringey asks all its departments to consider the following when contracting out services: 'Developing and putting into action mechanisms for embedding equalities in the process of tendering for council contracts . . ., developing and implementing a format for monitoring the take-up of services using Haringey's equalities categories, developing and implementing a format that incorporates performance in equal opportunities into the appraisal and evaluation of contractors' performance in providing services, promoting corrective measures where performance falls below specifications' (London Borough of Haringey 1995a: 11).

Organizations which resist change

One barrier to achieving change in equalities can be due to the way an organization operates. Many of the reasons have been summarized by

Blakemore and Drake: 'A number of reasons have been identified for the lack of centrality of equal opportunities in the world of management: ingrained patterns of institutional discrimination; organisational cultures which are swamped with economic and technological change and which cannot cope with yet more changes such as equal opportunity initiatives; and a clash between individualistic, competitive business values and a perception of equal opportunities as soft-hearted social justice' (1996: 204). However, none of these barriers are necessarily insurmountable. At a simple organizational level problems are likely if the policy itself is unclear or if there are ambiguities in the guidance notes relating to the policy. In some organizations there is little relation between policy and practice – this commonly occurs where policy is simply 'filed away'. An organization's culture may not be conducive to equalities work. An autocratic organization which does not recognize that opinions may differ will find it difficult to listen to the needs of different target groups. This has been described as resulting from an inability to develop a shared meaning of equalities: 'managers and staff tend to prefer prioritizing agreement rather than working through difference. The effects of this are that they do not learn how to work with and through difference, thereby limiting participation from disadvantaged groups. This creates and is sustained by an organizational dynamic' (Vince and Booth 1996: 9).

Vince and Booth argue that there are basically five different types of organizational culture, and that each deals with equalities in a different way. In most instances problems with equalities issues are likely to arise. Each of the five types of organization differs in its managerial commitment, its leadership values and in its response to change. The first type is the *Delusional Organization*. This is an organization where there is no commitment to equalities, no awareness of diversity and therefore no need for equalities work or for change. The second type of organization is the *Static Organization*. Here there are words but rarely action. There are policy statements but no implementation. Change does occasionally takes place but this usually occurs only when action is needed to stay within legal requirements. Initiatives on equalities are confined to employment issues and often left to inexperienced personnel staff. The third type is the *Parodic Organization*. Here the organization takes on the policies of other organizations without adapting them or understanding them. Equalities is seen as an 'image' issue. Minimum work is done, just enough to keep people quiet both within the organization and outside it. In this culture the organization has a basic policy on employment issues and has set up courses on equalities for managers in the hope that the message will be cascaded down the organization, but this does not happen. In the fourth type, the organization is characterized as *Active/Avoiding*. The organization has a 'confused commitment – manifested in both approaching and avoiding equality at the same time . . . It is desirable to work towards equality but "we don't want to open a can of worms" ' (Vince and Booth 1996: 11). Such an organization may have good policies but the arrangements for implementing them are incoherent. The fifth type is the *Learning Organization*. Here there is a 'long-term commitment to improving business by exploring relations among a diverse workforce' (ibid.: 11). Such an organization will value equal rights and equal outcomes. Its 'Strategic decision-making is linked to an acceptance of the emotion, power and paradox of policy development in a diverse workforce' (ibid.). This is the organization which understands equalities issues and is likely to act on them.

Vince and Booth argue that in any organization the best way to manage is through influence and persuasion rather than through formal procedures. Formal procedures are important but change is more likely to occur through 'networking' within the organization. For informal arrangements to work there needs to be a culture of communication coupled with feelings of trust among those who work on equalities: 'Mutual trust and supportive relationships appear central to collaborative success. Lack of trust inevitably implies the creation of very significant transaction costs through the imposition of formal contacts, and other detailed control mechanisms. Mutual trust based on reliability (partners do what they say they will do), cooperation (partners work together to sort problems out) and openness (partners share as much information as possible) is essential' (1996: 24). However, for informal collaborative work there needs to be agreed strategic objectives and good open communication. Networks that function outside clear, organization-wide policy can lead to cliques and intrigue and become counter-productive.

Resistance from staff

The rate and pace of change in an organization can be a barrier as well. So too can the culture of an organization. In relation to one example of equalities work, Weaver concluded that a particular measure had not been adopted because: 'Both the rate of change and the underlying ideology behind the changes are at odds with the development of responsible, appropriate, user-led services' (1996: 108). Change is always difficult and often even quite painful. The anxiety staff can feel about change is one reason why managers who attempt to implement equalities policies can encounter problems: 'Universalist policies designed to change behaviour within the organisation as a whole at all levels – of which equal opportunity policy is an example *par excellence* – are likely to face the most complex of problems in their implementation' (Young 1990: 31). Another reason why equalities work can be difficult to implement is because it will be seen as a threat by some factions as services are taken away from one group to ensure improved provision for others: 'In some circumstances widening opportunities for some unavoidably means reducing them for others. In other words, genuinely effective equality policies may have to hurt' (Blakemore and Drake 1996: 214). For those involved in equal opportunities work such changes take on an emotional component which can be difficult to cope with. In all involved, equal opportunities can bring to the fore feelings about race, disabled people, age and growing older, and relationship between the genders. Many of these issues are about power relations (see Chapter 2) and those included in decision making often feel uneasy when dealing with issues that might touch on their own sensitivity. For these reasons people are often uncomfortable dealing with equalities issues. Often the subject is seen as 'undiscussable': 'Thus there exists within the local authority context, as in most large organisations, a kind of in-built resistance to change created by traditional power relationships which must work against equal opportunity initiatives regardless of their structure, level of resources or policy orientation' (Stone 1988: 11). The level of personalization of policy discussion (as opposed to professionalism) is illustrated in a slightly different way as it relates to fairness. In one local authority, managers objected to any mention being made that the equalities target groups in the borough made up over 70 per cent of the population. Managers objected that this might upset 'white able-bodied men'. Most of the managers were themselves 'white able-bodied men'.

For all these reasons the most common problem when introducing equalities work is staff resistance. This expresses itself in many ways. Sometimes it is 'passive' resistance, where staff will say 'yes' but do little or nothing about the particular piece of work. This was the experience in one organization when equalities staff tried to implement equalities service reviews. Staff would delay the start of the project or not facilitate its initial progress. Some senior managers failed to embrace the changes fully and allowed the reviews to take place only in services that were seen as 'safe' and where minimal change would be needed. It is often difficult to predict where resistance will occur, partly because it is not easy to tell where the power is: 'All organisations have their own constantly shifting centres of power, both formal and informal, which determine the outcome of the decision-making process, but which are notoriously difficult to define. Even before the decision-making process begins, the centres of power within organisations "prefer" certain outcomes over others, and shifting these preferences towards the interests of those without power is a highly complicated and difficult task' (Stone 1988: 11). In her research Bagilhole (1993) found that 'some senior officers did find subtle ways to resist change. They continued to promote the old safer models of equal opportunities in opposition to the new more radical and political models. The policies they supported under the old models were those that were less threatening and less likely to effect change.' This often takes the form of promoting 'diversity' but not confronting discrimination. For example, in many organizations it is quite common to find a 'multicultural' attitude towards race issues whereby it is safe to 'celebrate' the diversity that exists among customers, but little is done to acknowledge racial discrimination and to look at the practices and procedures the organization may have which may well be discriminatory. This 'cultural diversity' view of race feels safe and unchallenging. It is also common to find organizations which feel 'safe' with one aspect of equalities work (usually race or gender) but not others: 'An example of this was the rigid and determined adherence to a cultural diversity perspective in the social services department. This perspective of race relations is difficult to argue against, and draws attention away from the department. It also ignores gender and disability' (Bagilhole 1993: 172). Resistance can also be more 'active', usually along the lines of 'We haven't got the resources', or 'We haven't got the time to do any more work.' In the case of one County Council, 'Equal opportunities was perceived as increasing the work-load, further limiting autonomy with increased bureaucracy, and therefore something to be circumvented if possible' (Bagilhole 1993: 171).

Resistance should not necessarily be seen as all negative. The fact that resistance occurs can be taken to mean that the work being done on equalities is becoming effective: 'In a way, resentment of, or resistance to, equality policies are a sign that they are beginning to bite. Purely cosmetic policies would excite little interest or controversy' (Blakemore and Drake 1996: 213). This certainly fits in with the author's experience. Equalities work is accepted by staff so long as it does not 'rock the boat' – as soon as it means real change, resistance sets in. Staff also feel resentful when 'outside forces' (another section or department) are asking for a change in the way they work. Adopting equalities may be seen as threatening their 'professional' status. Staff in a unit may feel that they know what their job is about and are not happy being told what they should do.

Another problem which leads to anxiety and resistance about equalities work is ignorance of, or misconceptions about, equal opportunities. Many staff feel they do not understand what equalities is about or how it works to bring about change. They feel 'panicked' at the thought of undertaking work with which they are unfamiliar and which they see as pointless. This can be overcome by making sure everyone involved is well informed through briefing sessions or training. This also means that when doing equalities work it is important to think through the process at the outset and ensure that the support needed for the work is available.

Another mechanism of resistance to equalities work which occurs is to allow projects to start but then let them fail. Not only is this demoralizing, but it also gives those who oppose the work the chance to feel justified in their opinion that it is a waste of time. At a higher level an organization might set up equalities systems to fail (by the failure to provide funding, resources, committee structure etc.).

Senior managers implementing equalities have often felt that one way of overcoming resistance is to get involved in equalities themselves. This works well if their role is to 'champion the issue'. But it can fail where they take responsibilities for implementing equalities away from other managers. The presence of senior managers in a team working towards implementation can make more junior staff feel 'gagged' and frightened to speak. It can therefore act as a barrier. This happened in local authorities where elected members got involved in day-to-day equalities work. Bagilhole found that senior officers resented 'close attention and involvement, as was shown in their discussion of this issue at management meetings. It was perceived by the officers as confusion over their and the elected members' respective roles. One effect of this was to negate senior officers' responsibilities for the policies' (1993: 171).

Equalities can meet resistance in local authorities when it becomes a political issue. This was relatively common in the 1980s when equal opportunities in service delivery was new. In a council those in 'opposition' may vote each year to abolish equalities work. In this type of climate, working in equalities is insecure and may not gain momentum. When a candidate was appointed as Head of Equalities in one local authority, the first thing she was told by one councillor from the opposition was that when they got back to power she would be sacked because 'equalities was not on (their) agenda'! When equal opportunities becomes a party political issue, implementation is more difficult and leads to frustration and bewilderment amongst officers. Opposition councillors may try to discredit equalities at committee or try to portray it as a trivial issue. This type of behaviour is not unique to local authorities. Often those in senior positions make it clear that they feel equalities is 'silly' or 'a waste of time' and try to undermine the work through ridicule or inertia. It is easy to ridicule someone working alone on equalities. It is much more difficult to ridicule a team. For this reason an organization that is seriously committed to equalities should have structures which will prevent victimization. Clear policy, commitment and supportive committee structure all help. These will usually lend weight to the decision-making process. A variety of actions can be taken to deal with tactics designed to undermine equalities. Some choose to ignore the opposition; alternatively it can be treated with disdain or attempts made to win it over. In one council when an opposition member made a long, angry and convoluted speech stating that he resented work on gay and lesbian issues because it was distasteful and immoral, a member of the Equalities Committee thanked him for sharing his personal feelings with the committee and the meeting moved on without further discussion. At other times it may be more appropriate to challenge the behaviour or respond in the understanding that the behaviour is due to a lack of awareness. One instance where awareness raising seemed to be the answer occurred where a court seemed unaware of the feelings of women experiencing violence. In response to this around 70 people from the voluntary and the statutory sector, and some individual women, arranged to meet three of the judges from the court. At the meeting the judges gave their view and the audience theirs. Women talked about how they experienced the process and agencies talked about their difficulties in the light of decisions the judges would make. It was clear that the judges had not recognized the problem and as a result of the meeting they resolved to change their practice. Such 'bridge building' meetings, if done with sensitivity, can be enormously influential. Hearings such as these can change organizations and even government.

Barriers to change can occur when people hold specific 'political' views. For example, some people believe that issues of race, gender, disability, age and sexuality are not real issues, but simply mask the fundamental problems in society which are due to class divisions: 'A dyed-in-the-wool socialist, for whom class is the fundamental and overriding social division which explains all other inequalities, might decry equal opportunities polices as a diversion from the "real" business of class conflict' (Blakemore and Drake 1996: 209). Another problem may occur when community activists see equal opportunities work done by large organizations as a means of undermining their own efforts: 'A radical feminist or black community activist would see equality strategies as yet another government ploy to buy off the leaders of their movements and to co-opt them into the establishment' (Blakemore and Drake 1996: 210). Some also oppose equalities work on the grounds that it interferes with civil liberties. Indeed, ensuring equality may mean reducing services to some groups and redistributing resources to others. It can also mean preventing people from harming others (e.g. injunctions taken out against individuals in cases of domestic violence or racial harassment). For these reasons it can happen that 'a right-winger who supports the free market and a libertarian who champions individual freedom would both oppose equal opportunities policies because they seem to represent gross interference with personal choice and the private life of the citizen' (Blakemore and Drake 1996: 110).

One method suggested for dealing with resistance is 'the force field techniques'. In this the protagonists for equalities would analyse support for, and resistance to, a particular piece of work. The method involves identifying those groups or individuals who support the project, those who resist it and those who are neutral. The measure of their support or resistance is also ascertained. The task then is to look at ways of strengthening those who support it, converting those who are neutral and looking at ways of reducing resistance (see LGMB 1991: 122). In all equalities work three things are crucial to success: negotiating between all those involved, ensuring that information flows between all parties, and making sure that the work does not drag on and lose momentum.

Resistance may come from the public

Much of this book stressed the importance for equalities work of public involvement and having work led by the needs of users and non-users. This brings with it problems to be overcome. It needs both individual negotiating skills and organizational structures to avoid introducing unnecessary tension. When discrimination or equalities has gone unchallenged for years, the public may feel they can no longer listen to offers of redress or efforts to involve them in improving services. The public simply 'don't want to know'. In attempts to improve relationships many local authorities set up forums to discuss equalities issues with local representatives from target groups. Some of these are successful, but many have failed. One reason for failure is because the establishment of the forum is, or is seen as, a gesture to keep the community quiet. This is particularly likely where the forum is controlled by the local authority and only concerned with the authority's agenda, and has no genuine consultative or participative mechanisms. Such forums are indeed a means of control and maintaining power. They could be seen as an example of where managers appeared to do something in order to do nothing. They are set up as a means of shutting up the community but offered as a process of consultation or set up to allow the public 'to let off steam'. In such a situation a community will no longer be willing to communicate meaningfully, which inevitably creates serious problems for equalities.

Conflict can arise when those in power feel threatened. It is important that managers are kept fully informed and recognize that in reality they may know less about people's needs than the people themselves. The following example of a participative event shows how good information flow can resolve conflict. Users of health care were part of a panel advising managers on training: 'early efforts proved disappointing. Managers felt threatened by the users' comments and reacted with hostility' (Moore 1995b). With perseverance and the continual flow of information matters resolved. The fear of managers was about loss of power. This occurs with many public involvement exercises where those in power feel it is their job at all levels to make decisions on behalf of people. Why then involve people? In reality, informed decisions are better decisions. Moreover, if decisions need to be justified, the more information the manager has, the more persuasive he or she will be. The point of public involvement is often to get information and gain understanding. Public involvement rarely involves loss of power although participative mechanisms do involve sharing power. The fear of a loss of power may be accompanied by fear that if one asks people for their views they will invariably ask for more than is possible and this raises expectations. Generally if a public involvement exercise is well planned and people are informed of its objectives and limitations, these fears do not materialize. People understand limitation on budgets.

In many public involvement exercises conflict is unavoidable as the needs of different people are likely to be conflicting. There will, for example, always be conflict between environmentalists and developers. A 'NIMBY (Not In My Back Yard)' attitude is inevitable. Anyone looking to consult on the opening of a hostel for the homeless will face angry residents wherever the hostel is to be situated. The important thing is to view conflict in a constructive manner. As Stewart says of local authorities and consultation: 'Voices, even if raised as they often are in protest, should not be regretted by a local authority but should be welcomed as part of active democracy. The aim should be however to turn protest towards discussion, so that all can understand the issues involved' (1995: 24). In some instances, even if the consultation shows that local people oppose an issue (a hostel for instance), the decision might still be made to go ahead. Views expressed by residents are important, but the overall need of the community at large (for a hostel) may be greater. This is common in the public sector: 'One of the key roles of local authorities is to reconcile or to balance the aspirations, demands and needs of the communities within. It is a mistake of those who stress the role of local authorities as community government or in community leadership to assume that there are necessarily shared interests and concerns. In reconciling differences and in balancing interests community leadership gains meaning' (Stewart 1995: 15). This involves recognizing that communities are diverse and therefore will have diverse and conflicting needs. In some cases where there are conflicting views between those involved, if these are not resolved decisions may be made regardless of people's views and on cost grounds alone. Rosie Weaver gives an example (1996: 104) in which mothers were consulted about the best timing for a baby clinic; some wanted it in the week, some in the evening, some at weekends. The final decision was made on cost grounds and resulted in the clinic opening on weekdays.

It is not necessary to fear conflict; conflict is often unavoidable because people have different needs. However, conflict can be minimized. Conflict and confrontation rarely resolve problems and are best avoided. Conflict can be reduced through careful planning of a public involvement exercise. Some public meetings often encourage a confrontational attitude. If an issue is known to be confrontational, use other methods by which people can air their views but where genuine discussion may take place, conflict may be negotiated, differences can be worked through and a consensus view be developed. It is easier to clarify the nature of any disagreement in a small group even if the group cannot resolve the problem. Recognizing different views and understanding their differences (seeing other people's point of view) is important in itself for conflict resolution since people will then have an understanding of opposing views and why theirs has not been adopted. Public involvement can be particularly difficult if, while seeking someone's views, the organization restricts the rights of people, as can happen with mental health problems, prisoners and parents whose children are taken into care. This does not mean that involvement should not occur in these situations; it can still be just as valid. It must be recognized that conflict is unavoidable. Excluding people is likely to make conflict worse. To avoid conflict it is important to learn to listen to other people's points of view, give support to those who have difficulty in expressing their views and allow people to get to know each other. Those who are seen as 'difficult' at meetings are often people who have not been listened to, are frustrated in not being able to express their views and 'find it difficult to be reasonable after years of being devalued and disempowered' (Beresford and Croft 1993: 137). They may feel that no one understands their view. According to Beresford and Croft (1993: 30–33), conflict can be minimized by being clear about the exercise; making it a positive experience for those involved; focusing discussion on the essential issues; not making assumptions; involving individual and collective discussion; linking help with listening (offering those involved information); working through people's personal agendas ('we should recognise the importance of allowing people the chance to express their personal concerns, however briefly, so they can get past them'); keeping people informed; not excluding people. A similar view advocates the following steps to minimize conflict:

- include all major interested parties
- participants (and not the authority) should accept responsibility for the programme
- people generally are kept informed
- a common definition of the problem is agreed
- in face-to-face situations, the participants educate each other
- decisions are made by consensus.

(Stewart 1995: 27)

It is important to reduce suspicion and mistrust of those carrying out public involvement exercises. To do this it helps to avoid duplicating the power relations that exist between provider and user in the exercise (e.g. avoid a 'them and us' type meeting with providers on a platform and users in rows facing them). Sometimes conflict is unavoidable because the service user is, through the exercise, playing the provider's game and fitting into the provider's arrangements, knowing that the provider will have the last word: 'They set the agenda, interpret the information and decide what to do with it. The dialogue that develops may be no more than *us* giving *them* our information and *them* telling *us* their decision' (Beresford and Croft 1993: 44). This can be lessened by more participative methods which give people some amount of power.

Whatever problems and barriers are faced it is important to keep them in perspective. Even in the midst of conflict, it is important to step back and remember what the work is about, and to remember that when policies fail it should not be taken at a personal level. It is rarely one individual's fault. But as said above, the issue can be an emotive one and so when working in this field one can easily feel hurt by failure and there will be those in the organization who will seek to personalize the failure or seek a scapegoat for mistakes. Everyone makes mistakes from time to time and things do not go smoothly all the time. Mistakes should be learnt from and not repeated. Equal opportunities in service delivery is never going to be easy but this does not mean that it is not worthwhile. It may simply take longer than one would hope but the rewards of such work are worth waiting for.

BIBLIOGRAPHY

Anlin, S. (1989) *Out but Not Down*. London: Homeless Action.

Association of London Government (ALG) (1997a) *Disability Equality: Achieving Access for All*. London: Association of London Government.

Association of London Government (ALG) (1997b) *Translators and Interpreters Services: A Handbook for Local Authorities*. London: Association of London Government.

Association of Metropolitan Authorities (AMA) (1993) *Local Authorities and Community Development: A Strategic Opportunity for the 1990s*. London: Association of Metropolitan Authorities.

Audit Commission (1993) *What Seems To Be the Matter: Communication between Hospitals and Patients*. London: HMSO.

Audit Commission (1997) *Local Authorities Performance Indicators*. London: DETR.

Bagilhole, B. (1993) Managing to be fair: implementing equal opportunities in a local authority. *Local Government Studies*, 19, 2: 163–75.

Ball, W. and Solomos, J. (1990) *Race and Local Politics*. London: Macmillan.

Barnes, M. and Prior, D. (1995) Spoilt for choice. *Public Money and Management*, July/September: 53–8.

Beresford, P. and Croft, S. (1993) *Citizen Involvement: A Practical Guide for Change*. Hampshire: Macmillan.

Blackburn, R. (ed.) (1993) *Rights of Citizenship*. London: Mansell Publishing.

Blakemore, K. and Drake, R. (1996) *Understanding Equal Opportunity Policies*. Hemel Hempstead: Prentice Hall.

Brindle, D. (1997) Disabled barred from most polling stations. *Guardian*, 16 July.

British Crime Survey (1994). London: Home Office.

Burton, P. (1993) *Community Profiling: A Guide to Identifying Local Needs*. Bristol: University of Bristol.

Business in the Community (1996) *Race for Opportunity: A Business in the Community Campaign Information Leaflet*. London: Business in the Community.

Bywaters, P. and McLeod, E. (eds) (1996) *Working for Equality in Health*. London: Routledge.

Carpenter, M. (1996) Beyond us and them: trade unions and equality in community care for users and workers. In P. Bywaters and E. McLeod (eds) *Working for Equality in Health*. London: Routledge.

City of Cardiff (1994) *Tenancy Agreements*. Cardiff: City of Cardiff Council.

Clark, F.A. (1992) Public awareness. *Total Quality Management*, December: 373–8.

Collier, J. and Collier, R. (1991) Detention of British citizens as hostages in the Gulf (letter). *British Medical Journal*, 303: 1405.

Collier, R. (1994) *Watch Your Language: A Guide to Writing in Gender Neutral Terms.* London: City Centre Project.

Commission for Racial Equality (CRE) (1995a) *Age and Race: Double Discrimination. Life in Britain Today for Ethnic Minority Elders.* London: CRE and Age Concern.

Commission for Racial Equality (CRE) (1995b) *Annual Report.* London: CRE.

Commission for Racial Equality (CRE) (1995c) *Kick it Again: Uniting Football Against Racism.* London: CRE.

Commission for Racial Equality (CRE) (1995d) *Race for Opportunity.* London: CRE.

Commission for Racial Equality (CRE) (1995e) *Racial Equality Means Business: A Standard for Racial Equality for Employers.* London: CRE.

Commission for Racial Equality (CRE) (1995f) *Racial Equality Means Quality.* London: CRE.

Commission for Racial Equality (CRE) (1996a) *Action on Racial Harassment: A Guide for Multi-Agency Panels.* London: CRE.

Commission for Racial Equality (CRE) (1996b) *Annual Report.* London: CRE.

Commission for Racial Equality (CRE) (1996c) *Connections* No. 7. London: CRE.

Commission for Racial Equality (CRE) (1996d) *1996 at the CRE.* London: CRE.

Commission for Racial Equality (CRE) and Equal Opportunities Commission (EOC) (1996) *Further Education and Equality.* London and Manchester: CRE and EOC.

Commission for Racial Equality (CRE), Equal Opportunities Commission (EOC) and Committee of Vice-Chancellors and Principals (CVCP) (1997) *Higher Education and Equality: A Guide.* London and Manchester: CRE, EOC and CVCP.

Community Development Foundation (CDF) (1995) *Regeneration and the Community: Guidelines to the Community Involvement Aspects of the SRB Challenge Fund.* London: CDF.

Coote, A. and Campbell, B. (1987) *Sweet Freedom.* Oxford: Blackwell.

Croydon Domestic Violence Joint Planning Team (1997) *Croydon Inter-Agency Protocol on Domestic Violence.* London: Croydon Domestic Violence Joint Planning Team.

Daniels, A. (1997) Airline apology for bad form. *Guardian*, 30 July.

Delin, A. (1997) Cereal numbers. Diary of a disability campaigner. *Guardian*, 27 August.

Department of the Environment (DoE) (1994) *Partnership in Practice.* London: DoE.

Department of the Environment (DoE) (1995) *Involving Communities in Urban and Rural Regeneration: A Guide for Practitioners.* London: DoE.

Department of the Environment, Transport and the Regions (DETR) (1997) *Draft paper on Best Value Pilot Scheme.* London: DETR.

Department of Health (DoH) (1995) *The Patient's Charter.* London: DoH.

Disabled Persons' Transport Advisory Committee (DPTAC) (1995) *Meeting the Needs of Disabled Passengers: Advice for Taxi Drivers.* London: DPTAC.

Donaldson, L. (1995) Sounding so insecure. *Guardian*, 16 August.

Douglas, J. (1996) Developing with black and minority ethnic communities health promotion strategies which address social inequalities. In P. Bywaters and E. McLeod (eds) *Working for Equality in Health.* London: Routledge.

Egerton, J. (1994) Out but not down: lesbian experience of housing. In M. Evans, *The Woman Question.* London: Sage.

Employer's Forum on Disability (1996) *Marks and Spencer: Welcoming Disabled Customers.* London: Employer's Forum on Disability.

Employment Department Group (1995) *Equal Opportunities: Ten Point Plan for Employers.* London: Employment Department Group.

English Heritage (1995a) *Easy Access to Historic Properties.* London: English Heritage.

English Heritage (1995b) *Guide for Visitors with Disabilities.* London: English Heritage.

Equalities News (Local Government Information Unit) (1996) Racial harassment powers. 27: 2.

Equalities News (Local Government Information Unit) (1997) Invisible women. 28: 9.
Equal Opportunities Commission (EOC) (1991) *Equal Opportunities Makes Good Business Sense*. Manchester: EOC.
Equal Opportunities Review (1995) Race policy not being translated into action. 60: 16–19.
Equal Opportunities Review (1997) Improving equality law: the options. 72: 28–34.
Evans, M. (1994) *The Woman Question*. London: Sage.
Friedan, B. (1963) *The Feminine Mystique*. London: Penguin.
Friedan, B. (1994) *The Fountain of Age*. London: Vintage.
Gas Care News (1995/1996)
Gas News (1994) Equal opportunities: from ideas to action. May: 6–7.
Graham, H. (1996) Researching women's health work: a study of the lifestyles of women on income support. In P. Bywaters and E. McLeod (eds) *Working for Equality in Health*. London: Routledge.
Greater London Council (GLC) (1986a) *Danger! Heterosexism at Work. A Handbook on Equal Opportunities in the Workplace for Lesbians and Gay Men*. London: Greater London Council.
Greater London Council (GLC) (1986b) *Women's Handbook*. London: Greater London Council.
Health Which? (1995) The welfare plate: meals-on-wheels food. December: 206–9.
Institute for Public Policy Research (IPPR) (1993) *Social Justice in a Changing World*. London: Institute of Public Policy and Research.
Jones, A. (1996) *Making Monitoring Work: A Handbook for Racial Equality Practitioners*. Warwick: Centre for Research in Ethnic Relations.
Kandola, R., Fullerton, J. and Ahmed, Y. (1995) Managing diversity: succeeding where equal opportunities has failed. *Equal Opportunities Review*, 50: 31–6.
Kennedy, H. (1993) *Eve was Framed: Women and British Justice*. London: Virago.
Leach, B. (1989) Disabled people and the implementation of local authority equal opportunities policies. *Public Administration*, 67: 65–77.
Local Government Association (1997) *Equalities Indicators and Key Definitions. Report to Equal Opportunities Panel in June*. London: Local Government Association.
Local Government Information Unit (LGIU) (1991a) *New Directions in Local Government: Going for Quality*. London: LGIU.
Local Government Information Unit (LGIU) (1991b) *Priority for Equality: Report of a Conference on Local Government and Equal Opportunities*. London: LGIU.
Local Government Information Unit (LGIU) (1995) *Equality: A Report of the LGIU Conference on Managing Council Performance on Equality*. London: LGIU.
Local Government Information Unit (LGIU) (1996) *Disability Discrimination Act 1995: A Guide for Local Authorities*. London: LGIU.
Local Government Management Board (LGMB) (1991) *Quality and Equality: Service to the Whole Community*. London: LGMB.
Local Government Management Board (LGMB) (1992) *Leadership and Quality Management*. London: LGMB.
Local Government Management Board (LGMB) (1996a) *Equalities and the Contract Culture*. Luton: LGMB.
Local Government Management Board (LGMB) (1996b) *Equalities and Organisational Design*. Luton: LGMB.
London Borough of Croydon (1997a) *A Guide to Service Reviews and Standards*. London: London Borough of Croydon.
London Borough of Croydon (1997b) *Community Involvement*. London: London Borough of Croydon.
London Borough of Croydon (1997c) *Equalities Commitment* (leaflets). London: London Borough of Croydon.

London Borough of Croydon (1997d) *Monitoring Equalities in Service Delivery*. London: London Borough of Croydon.

London Borough of Haringey (1991) *Organisational Development of Equal Opportunities*. London: London Borough of Haringey.

London Borough of Haringey (1995a) *From the Margins to the Mainstream: Equalities Audit*. London: London Borough of Haringey.

London Borough of Haringey (1995b) *From the Margins to the Mainstream: Equal Opportunities Policy Document*. London: London Borough of Haringey.

London Borough of Hounslow (1990) *Racial Harassment: A Corporate Policy and Guidelines to Departments*. London: London Borough of Hounslow.

London Borough of Hounslow (1993) *STEPS Guide: Strategic Equality Plans in Service Delivery*. London: London Borough of Hounslow.

London Borough of Hounslow (1994a) *Going Public: Involving the Community in the Work of the Council*. London: London Borough of Hounslow.

London Borough of Hounslow (1994b) *Factsheet for Frontline Staff Responding to Queries on Equal Opportunities in Service Delivery*. London: London Borough of Hounslow.

London Borough of Hounslow (1994c) *Residents' Survey*. London: London Borough of Hounslow.

London Borough of Hounslow (1995) *Spelling it Out*. London: London Borough of Hounslow.

London Borough of Hounslow (1996a) *Counting on Equality*. London: London Borough of Hounslow.

London Borough of Hounslow (1996b) *Hounslow Against Ageism*. London: London Borough of Hounslow.

London Housing Unit (1991) *Cutting it Out: Sexual Harassment*. London: London Housing Unit.

London Research Centre (LRC) (1997) *Asian Housing Needs in Croydon*. London: LRC.

London Strategic Policy Unit (LSPU) (1987) *People Like Us: Lesbians and Gays in the Community*. London: LSPU.

McDowell, L. and Pringle, R. (1992) *Defining Women*. Cambridge: Polity Press.

Maguire, A. (1992) Power: Now you see it, now you don't. In L. McDowell and R. Pringle (eds) *Defining Women*. Cambridge: Polity Press.

Mair, N. (1992) On being a cripple. In L. McDowell and R. Pringle (eds) *Defining Women*. Cambridge: Polity Press.

Marks and Spencer (1996) *Equal Opportunities and You: A Guide for All Staff*. London: Marks and Spencer plc.

Marshall, T. H. (1950) *Citizenship and Social Class and Other Essays*. Cambridge: Cambridge University Press.

Massie, B. (1994) *Disabled People and Social Justice*. London: Institute for Public Policy Research.

Modood, T. (1994) *Racial Equality: Colour, Culture and Justice*. Institute for Public Policy Research.

Modood, T. (1997) *Britain's Ethnic Minorities: Diversity and Disadvantage*. London: Institute for Public Policy Research.

Modood, T., Berthold, R., Lakey, J. *et al.* (1997) *Ethnic Diversity in Britain: Diversity and Disadvantage*. London: Policy Studies Institute.

Moore, W. (1995a) All hands to the slump. *Guardian*, 24 May.

Moore, W. (1995b) Lessons from the bedside. *Guardian*, 6 June.

Morris, P. (1995) Community council. *Municipal Journal*, 46: 24–5.

O'Neill, D. (1996) Health care for older people: ageism and equality. In P. Bywaters and E. McLeod (eds) *Working for Equality in Health*. London: Routledge.

Pearce, S. (1995) Defining equality and service provision. In *Equality: A Report of the LGIU Conference*. London: Local Government Information Unit.

Percy-Smith, J., Hawton, M. and Hughes, G. (1994) *Community Profiling: Auditing Social Needs*. Buckingham: Open University Press.

Phillips, A. (1992) Feminism, equality and difference. In L. McDowell and R. Pringle, *Defining Women*. Cambridge: Polity Press.

Phillips, A. (1993) *Democracy and Difference*. Cambridge: Polity Press.

Prior D., Stewart J. and Walsh K. (1995) *Citizenship: Rights, Community and Participation*. London: Pitman Publishing.

Quiller Press (1996) *Access in London*. London: Quiller Press.

Read, J. and Wallcroft, J. (1995) *Guidelines for Equal Opportunities and Mental Health*. London: MIND and UNISON.

Ross, R. and Schneider, R. (1992) *From Equality to Diversity: Business Case for Equal Opportunity*. London: Pitman Publishing.

Royal National Institute for the Blind, Employers Forum on Disability, Scope and British Gas (1997) *Good Practice, Great Business. Disability in Business*. London: RNIB.

Scope (1996) *Disabled in Britain: A World Apart*. London: Scope.

Seeboard (1995) *Services for Customers Who Are Elderly or Disabled or Have Special Needs*. West Surrey: Seeboard.

Smith, P. (1997) *In Search of Solutions to the Problems of Exclusions: A Report for the London Borough of Croydon*. London: London Borough of Croydon.

Stewart, J. (1995) *Innovation in Democratic Practice*. Birmingham: Institute of Local Government Studies.

Stewart, J., Kendall, E. and Coote, A. (1994) *Citizens' Juries*. London: Institute for Public Policy Research.

Stone, I. (1988) *Equal Opportunities in Local Authorities*. London: HMSO.

Stonewall (1997) *Vote for Equality: A Gay and Lesbian Guide to the General Election*. London: Stonewall.

Stroke Association (1996) *Sex after Stroke Illness*. Leaflet No. S16. London: Stroke Association.

Sutton, G.C. (1997) Will You Still Need Me, Will You Still Screen Me When I'm Past 64? *British Medical Journal*, 25 October.

Thomas, D. and Ely, R. (1996) Making difference matter: a new paradigm for managing diversity. *Harvard Business Review*, September/October: 79–90.

UNISON (1995) *Unison Guide*. London: UNISON.

United Nations (1995) *United Nations 4th World Conference on Women: Action for Equality, Development and Peace*. New York: United Nations.

University of Central Lancashire (1993) *Equal Opportunities Policy Statement and Code of Practice*. Preston: University of Central Lancashire.

University of North London (1990) *Equal Opportunities for All: Policy and Action*. London: University of North London.

Vince, R. and Booth, C. (1996) *Equalities and Organisational Design*. London: Local Government Management Board.

Weaver, R. (1996) Localities and inequalities: local management in the inner city. In P. Bywater and E. McLeod (eds) *Working for Equality in Health*. London: Routledge.

Westminster City Council (1997) *Corporate Disability Policy* and accompanying *Council Report*. London: Westminster City Council.

Wilcox, D. (1994) *The Guide to Effective Participation*. Brighton: Partnership Books.

Young, K. (1990) Approaches to Policy Development in the Field of Equal Opportunities. In W. Ball and J. Solomos (eds) *Race and Local Politics*. London: Macmillan.

Young, S. (1996) *Promoting Participation and Community-Based Partnerships in the Context of Local Agenda 21: A Report for Practitioners*. Manchester: University of Manchester.

INDEX

COMBATING SEXUAL HARASSMENT IN THE WORKPLACE

Rohan Collier

Sexual harassment is common, hurtful to the recipient and wasteful to employers. It has to be tackled by employers and workers alike. This book offers insight from both sides as well as providing solutions. It asks:

- Why does sexual harassment occur?
- How can organizations prevent sexual harassment and deal with it?
- What is the legal standing of all parties involved?

It provides practical advice for managers, personnel officers and trade unionists on developing and implementing sexual harassment policies. In plain English this book provides a background to current legislation (including the European Union's Code of Practice) and UK practice, outlining recent developments. The author, who has many years experience in dealing with harassment issues, gives a detailed analysis of the reasons why harassment occurs, arguing that sexual harassment has more to do with power relations than with sexuality.

Contents

Introducing and defining sexual harassment – Sexism and sexual harassment – The legal challenge – Protecting the dignity of women and men at work: the EC Code of Practice – Developing sexual harassment policies – Trade unions, the Equal Opportunities Commission and advice agencies – Sexual harassment training in practice – Appendices – Bibliography – Index.

176pp   0 335 19082 0 (Paperback)

MAKING GENDER WORK
MANAGING EQUAL OPPORTUNITIES

Jenny Shaw and Diane Perrons (eds)

Making Gender Work analyses both the broad economic, legal and cultural frame-
works of equal opportunities and assembles first-hand accounts from pioneers in
the field. This integration of academic and practical expertise represents a major
contribution to the management of equal opportunities and analysis of organizations.

For a growing number of people gender *is* their work whilst, for others, it is the
reason why they get less (or more) pay, training and recognition *at* work. This
book is a response both to the rise of jobs or careers in equal opportunities and to
the conditions which make such jobs necessary. Both trends indicate that gender
expertise needs to become professionalized and not remain a purely academic or
analytical skill. This book indicates how those skills might be developed and the
sort of broad background knowledge practitioners will need if they are to be
effective change agents.

Contents
*Introduction – Part 1: The socio-economic, legal and cultural context of gender work –
Recent changes in women's employment in Britain – The economics of equal opportunities – The role of the law in equal opportunities – Employment deregulation and equal
opportunities – Towards a family-friendly employer – Organizational culture and
equalities work – Part 2: Managing equal opportunities: practical issues – Women in the
public and voluntary sectors – Working within local Government – Implementing equal
opportunities in a local authority – Equal opportunities and the voluntary sector – Trade
unions and equal opportunities – The appeal and the claims of non-dominant groups –
Conclusion – References – Index.*

Contributors
Helen Brown, Paul Burnett, Linda Clarke, Rita Donaghy, Lisa Harker, Margaret
Hodge, Sally Holtermann, Carole Pemberton, Diane Perrons, Jenny Shaw, Gillian
Stamp and Ruth Valentine.

256pp   0 335 19365 X (Paperback)   0 335 19366 8 (Hardback)